Juicy Fruit

CHRISTIANITY

JUICY FRUIT - CHRISTIANITY
Kerry L. George

International Standard Book Number:
0-9716449-8-5

Printed in the United States of America

CHRISTIANITY

R.L. George

To my Jesus, my Savior and my God, of whom I could never say enough. You served the sentence for me so that I could have life and life more abundantly. You have empowered me in my life through Your Holy Spirit for victory and freedom. May this book point only to You, and glorify Your Holy Name. May You cause it to be a blessing to all who read it, that they will bear good juicy fruit. I love You my Lord.

Amen.

Contents

Contents

ONE

There Are Signs

A s I began to think, plan and pray about writing this book I had to ask myself, "What do I have that I could share that people would be interested in?" I am not a famous person, nor am I a fabulously wealthy entrepreneur, nor am I a pastor of a church that seats six thousand people. No, by the world's standards I have done very little that is noteworthy. However, when you meet me I think that you would notice something different. Not everybody sees it, but many do.

It is not that I am so great, eloquent or charismatic. It is none of those things. I am not so pious and holy that I cannot be approached. I think that I am probably fairly ordinary to look at. I am of average height and a bit overweight. So it is definitely not my appearance that makes me appealing, but you would most likely be attracted to me anyway. Many people are. In fact, strangers often talk to me. They even bear the most intimate secrets of their heart to me.

I do not have a perfect life either. Many things have gone wrong and I have seen numerous trials and tribulations. According to the society that surrounds me I should be the most defeated person in my neighborhood. You see, I am a single mother of three children. But I am not worn out and run ragged; I am not without hope. In fact, I home school my eldest son while looking after the others. I pastor a new church in a small town in rural Canada, and I take my own college education through a distance learning program. I am a very busy person, but I am not harried and frazzled like some busy people that you may know.

If you met me, you would probably notice that I have a bounce to my step and a twinkle in my eye. You would also likely notice that I have a quick laugh that rolls out spontaneously, and you might even have a good laugh too! (Even if you were not intending to, or even if you had not had a good laugh in a long, long time.)

Sometimes people come under conviction around me. This is not always as much fun as the laughter, but it is a good thing as well. As a result many people get healed, saved and set free. There is a power in my testimony and a strength in my walk, and there is JOY, JOY, JOY!

Am I bragging? Not at all. The reason that I am telling you all of this is because it has not always been this way. I want to encourage you if you are not yet experiencing the things that I am telling you about. I want to lift you up and tell you that you can live this way too, if you want to. God will do for you what He has done for me. He says in His Word that He does not pick any favorites. So, the victory that I have in my life you can have as well.

Then Peter opened his mouth and said: "In truth I perceive that God shows no partiality."
- Acts 10:34

But before I tell you more about what I have now, let me tell you what I used to be like. That will give you hope. When you see the depths that I have been lifted up from (or the hole under the rock that I crawled out of), you will surely be encouraged.

You see, I used to be a defeated, wimpy, wishy-washy, "mamsey-pamsey" Christian. Nobody ever got saved coming around me. I was a hypocrite. I had a small relationship with Jesus. I mean, I loved Him, and He loved me, so what more was there to it? I went to church on Sundays, and for some periods I even attended a midweek Bible study, but I never really let Christ follow me home afterwards. Well, He was there in my heart I guess, but kind of squashed down. It was like I was telling Him, "Okay God, You had Your two hours on Sunday morning, now don't try to get out of Your box!"

I pretty much continued to do things like I always had done them. I read the newspaper a lot, as well as some science fiction and the occasional romantic epic. I watched two to four hours a day of television. I listened to some country music and a little rock and roll. I often went out singing karaoke or dancing at a nightclub on Saturday nights, but I never really got very drunk, and I always got up and went to church the next day, so what is the big deal anyway?

I had one foot in the church and one foot in the world, but they were my feet and I was going to do what I wanted. So there!

But, was I happy?

No. Definitely not.

You see, that was the kicker. I was doing everything that I wanted to do, but if it was making me so happy, then why did I sometimes cry myself to sleep at night all wrapped up in the fetal position? Why did I have pangs of guilt over the drinking and partying and all of the other things that went with it? (I do not think I need to get into what those things are. If you have ever partied, you know what they are. If you have never lived that lifestyle, you are better off not knowing about the details.) So if I was so right about my life's choices, why was I so unhappy in my circumstances?

There was something else that was bothering me. One time I listened to a man in my church give his testimony and talk about all of the people he had recently led to Jesus. I began to realize that I never impacted people that way. Sometimes I had good intentions, but I would often end up either joining the person in their sin, or being hurt by those that I tried to help.

4

Once, I met a young woman at social services who desperately needed a place to stay. Wanting to help her, I had taken her home with me and given her the use of a spare bedroom in my house. Over the next few weeks I watched helplessly as she slept with over thirty men, ran my phone bill up to $800, and even held a coke party at my home while I was away for the weekend. I was powerless to help her, and it irritated me. The only thing that I could do was ask her to move out for my own safety.

Some Christians that I knew seemed to be living much like I was. They may not have been involved in the same sin that I was involved in, but they did seem to be pretty powerless. They often were sick and snivelly throughout the winter months, they complained of poor finances and unfair taxes... and they did not seem to be leading anyone to the Lord, either. "Maybe this is all there is," I thought.

Then a very nice lady from my church met me at my workplace one afternoon and asked if I could join her for a coffee break. I was already impressed that such a professionally dressed and put-together woman would seek me out for friendship, but then she proceeded to explain that the Lord had given her a "word" for me. I found that part even more exciting! No one had ever given me a "word" before and I could not wait to hear what the Lord wanted to tell me. Maybe I was going to be suddenly blessed with lots of money, or maybe He just wanted to tell me how pleased He was with me. I was giddy with anticipation as we sat down in a quiet spot over two cups of steaming beverages.

First we chatted briefly, for I hardly knew her. She was an associate pastor at the church that I attended, and although I saw her there from time to time we had never sat down for a private discussion before. After a few moments she reached out and covered my hand with hers. I will never forget her piercing green eyes as she looked into the windows of my soul.

"God loves you Kerry, and He has a plan and a purpose for your life."

"Yes," I thought, eagerly leaning forward.

"But," she continued, "He has seen the sin that you have tried to hide."

With her gaze still penetrating deep into my hidden mind I felt my face heating up and turning alarmingly red. I shifted nervously, suddenly wanting to get away, or to strike back and defend myself, but I could not move. It was as though an unseen force had pinned me to my chair and I was unable to choke out even a sound.

"Do not be deceived," she said. "God will not be mocked, for whatever a man sows, that he will also reap. For he who sows, to his flesh will reap corruption, but he who sows to the Spirit will of the Spirit reap everlasting life." She had quoted those words from Galatians and now she released my hand to remove a small Bible that she had brought with her. As she opened it I wanted to run, but was deflated, like all of the wind had left my sails and I was stuck drifting on a lifeless sea awaiting some impending doom. I just sat there shaking and sputtering, caught in a trap of my own iniquity.

Then she began to read to me, explaining as she went. "Now the works of the flesh are evident, which are adultery," she paused, and I gulped. "Fornication - that is sexual sin and perversions like pornography, sexual fantasies, sex outside of wedlock, sexual talk and innuendoes," she stared intently at me as she spoke and I knew the shame I wore on my face. "Uncleanness," a pause, "lewdness - that is foul language and any speech that does not glorify Jesus or lift up His saints," she waited as I blinked back tears struggling to regain my composure. "Idolatry - that is putting people, time, money, jobs, kids, or anything in a place of more importance than Jesus. If you want to know who has most of your time check your schedule, and if you want to know who has most of your money look at your check book."

For a second I thought that she had actually seen those things, but I knew that she had not. "Sorcery," she said pausing again.

"At least I am not doing that," I thought.

"Hatred...."

"Ouch."

"Contentions," she said.

I was glad that I did not know what that one meant.

"Jealousies..."

"Don't have that one," I thought.

"Outbursts of wrath..."

"Oooooh," ' Conviction was hitting me in waves by this point. I was not even really hearing her as she went on and on and on.

"Selfish ambitions, dissensions, heresies, envy, murders, drunkenness, revelries, and the like; of which I tell you beforehand, just as I also told you in time past..."

She stopped to gain my attention again. As I looked into her face she spoke echoing into my very being, "...that those who practice such things will not inherit the kingdom of God!"

The weight of those words hit me like a concrete slab. My breath left me in violent bursts and I began to sob uncontrollably. I felt suddenly exposed as though I were naked before a mob of onlookers. I wondered, "Who else knows?" Then I realized that it did not matter who else knew. God knew. He had seen my sin and there was nowhere to hide from His eyes. He could see into my living room, my bedroom and even worse, into the thoughts of my heart.

Shaken as I was from that experience, that alone did not change me. Oh, I thank God that she had the boldness to confront me and give me that "word". It must have been really hard for her to do. She probably watched me afterwards to see if it sunk in, and for many months she and the Lord watched me with sadness. But a seed had been planted. I wanted to change. I wanted to change so badly. I just did not know how. I did not know where to start. It seemed as though my problems were so many and I was powerless over my own flesh.

I knew I had to change, but it still took some time for me to come to the end of myself. I had to fail some more before I would finally give up control over my life. I had to fall on my face really hard before I looked up. However, when I did, it was a complete work. I stepped down a life-changing fork in the road that I have never since regretted.

At last, I gave my life to Jesus Christ. Not just a little bit of it either. I gave Him the whole thing. I did not pray some weak, wimpy, little prayer that I meant with only half my heart. No. I cried out in desperation to the Living God and I told Him that I would follow Him every way He told me to. I told Him that I was going to listen and learn from His Word because I felt like I was going to die if I did not. I was so hungry, so ready, and so willing. I surrendered everything to Him.

Are you ready to give it all? Are you fed up with lack, misery, defeat, hopelessness, anger, no self-control, perversion and garbage in your life? Are you looking for answers to questions that nobody can help you with? Are you struggling with guilt and bondage to sin and habits that seem totally out of your power to deal with?

Then I encourage you—before we go any further in this book—let's get right with God. Let's get real with Him. He can see right into the depths of your soul and you cannot hide from Him anyway. He saw the sin that you did today, yesterday and last week. It did not surprise Him. He knew about it before you even did it. So let's not sneak around in our sin anymore. Let's face it squarely.

Maybe you have asked Jesus into your heart before. So had I but my life was not transformed until I gave Him everything.

Have you been transformed? Are you walking in victory? Is there good fruit on your tree? Are you impacting people for the gospel on a regular basis? How many souls did you personally lead to Jesus in the last year? If you can answer these questions positively and honestly without getting defensive then you are probably living a victorious life already, and have no need of this book. Give it to someone else that needs it. But if you are getting the least bit squeamish or convicted, or if you have the urge to throw this book into the nearest incinerator, then you are very likely in need of what I have to share. There is nobody that knows your thoughts except you and God. Can you get honest with Him right now?

If you have already been transformed and you are walking in victory and power, then you will know what I am talking about. However, if any one of the fruit of the Spirit is lacking in your life and you are not walking in victory, check your heart. What are you holding back? Define it, then hand it over to Jesus.

Let's do this right now. Why wait? Today is the day of your salvation! Pray this prayer with me right now.

"Heavenly Father, help me. I am so lost and defeated. I have tried to do it my own way and I have botched it all up. I have put people, activities, work and even television in a place that is more important than You. I have sinned against You in many ways, and You have seen it. Oh Lord, forgive me. I ask Jesus to come into my life right now and to change me. I am not even near perfect and I need You to transform me by Your power so that my life becomes a testimony for You."

"Set me free from everything that binds me, I ask You now in the Name of Jesus. Wash me in the precious blood of Jesus and cleanse away every sin and every desire to sin. Lord, I ask You to shine a light on every aspect of my life, and should You expose any improper motives of my heart, may You cause me to repent quickly and not harbor that sin any longer."

"Lord help me to know Your voice and to respond to Your leading. God, I do not want to move any longer unless I know it is by Your prompting and leading. I give every decision to You. If I am not sure that it is Your will for my life then I will put off making a decision until You confirm Your plan for me through Your Word or Your people."

"Father, I give You my heart, my life, my finances, my family and everything that I have. It is Yours—for Your service and Your glory. I choose to follow Jesus now. I choose to read His Word daily. I choose to pray daily. Oh God, transform me according to Your plan and purpose for my life. I choose to be obedient to Your will and to allow You to take over every aspect of my life. From now on I will do whatever Your Word tells me to do. I will act upon Your conviction in my spirit. I am going to receive Your correction and repent, and turn away completely from every sin that You convict me of."

"Holy Spirit, come and fill me up full to overflowing. Pour Your anointing through me like waves of oil washing over and through me. Holy Spirit, I invite

You to take over and change me. Transform me and empower me to be all that You want me to be."

"I ask all of these things in the Name of Jesus, and I receive them by faith. Glory to Your Holy Name. I exalt You, oh Lord. Amen."

Well, your transformation has begun. There are angels in heaven rejoicing and celebrating over your salvation and your commitment right now. Your journey has started and today is the first day of the rest of your life. I encourage you to write out that prayer and over the coming weeks repeat it to yourself to remind yourself of what you have given to the Lord.

Now, in the next few chapters I am going to share some of the things that He has just given to you and how to walk in them. I will show you how God can take a plain ordinary person such as you or me, and change us into an extraordinary testimony of His power and grace that can impact the world around us!

TWO

Filled, Filled, Filled

The evening that I got down on my knees and gave my whole life over to Jesus everything began to change. Suddenly it was the easiest thing in the world to follow Him. There were no more questions. If I found it in the Word then I believed it and I did it. It was that simple.

I began to read the Bible with zeal. I would stay up late, absorbing every line. Sometimes I would wake up in the middle of the night at the Holy Spirit's prompting, and sit and sing praises to the Lord. I would worship, pray and read the Word until the wee hours of the night. The amazing thing was that I would awake refreshed in the morning as though I had slept more than my usual eight hours.

At this point I had received the Holy Spirit and was learning to listen to Him. He would sometimes speak to me quietly, and as I harkened to Him I began to hear Him more audibly. He began to guide me in decision making, and again, as I obeyed Him things quickly got better in my life.

One immediate change was that I now had hope. I also had life. Lots of life. Lots of energy. In fact, I had energy to burn. I was so excited that I could barely sit still. Frequently I would wake up from a sound sleep because I was just too happy!

But did you know that there is a difference between receiving the Holy Spirit and being filled with the Holy Spirit? Yes there is! I was excited and happy but I was not yet empowered to share the gospel. However, I had yielded to Jesus totally and so He quickly made a way for me to be filled with the Holy Spirit just like He did for His disciples.

> *So Jesus said to them again, "Peace to You! As the Father has sent Me, I also send you." And when He had said this, He breathed on them, and said to them, "Receive the Holy Spirit."*
>
> *- John 20:21*

Jesus had already been resurrected when He told them this, and they did indeed receive the Holy Spirit as He breathed on them. However, they were not yet filled, because He later told them,

"But you shall receive power when the Holy Spirit has come upon you; and you shall be witnesses to Me in Jerusalem, and in all Judea and Samaria, and to the end of the earth."
- Acts 1:8

The disciples had clearly received the Holy Spirit in John 20:21, however they did not receive the power to proclaim the gospel until the Holy Spirit came upon them and filled them to overflowing later, on the day of Pentecost.

And they were all filled with the Holy Spirit and began to speak with other tongues, as the Spirit gave them utterance..
- Acts 2:4

Like the disciples, I had experienced an encounter with the Lord as I had surrendered to Him, and received the Holy Spirit. However, I was not yet empowered to share the gospel, nor was I filled to overflowing. This is important to mention, because unless a believer is continually filled and indwelt by the Holy Ghost it is impossible for them to live a victorious life. That is why we often meet Christians who may exhibit some of the gifts of the

Spirit while they do not manifest all of the fruit of the Spirit. (There will be more of this in Chapter 3.)

Sometimes the Lord will send His servants to lay hands on a believer to receive the Holy Spirit and be filled at the same time. That is what happened to Saul of Tarsus.

> *And Ananias went his way and entered the house; and laying his hands on him he said, "Brother Saul, the Lord Jesus, who appeared to you on the road as you came, has sent me that you may receive your sight and be filled with the Holy Spirit."*
>
> *- Acts 9:17*

This is done in many churches across our land and it is Scriptural. However, this is not the only way that the Holy Spirit can descend upon a person and fill them up. God is not limited. He came in Acts chapter two upon a place at a certain time and filled all those who were there. That is what happened to me.

Within days of my inner transformation a husband and wife asked me to join them in their prayer and deliverance ministry. That alone was a miracle. Nobody could have known what was going on in my relationship with Jesus because I had sinned openly before the world only weeks before. They did not know me well, but they did know me well enough to recognize that I had been a hypocrite. Even so, they came to me and said that God had shown them in a vision that I was to join them as they prayed for the sick in our community. I had never heard anyone talk about seeing visions from the Lord and at first wondered if they were missing a few screws. But I had given my life to Jesus and I decided I would pray about this decision like I had promised my Lord.

As I laid it to prayer I had a strong prompting from the Holy Spirit that this opportunity was of Him. I felt Him telling me to go with them for a season of training.

The first time we got together it was a Friday night. There were seven people gathered together in a basement living room of a house in Edmonton, Alberta. We started the evening by watching an awesome video about the Holy Spirit. We all watched, amazed, as people in a large auditorium fell out of their seats by the hundreds, and even flipped over backwards as they were approached by an anointed man of God. I had never heard of such a thing and I found it astonishing. We then spent time together praying and worshipping the Lord. Two hours slipped by quickly and the presence of God became thick and sweet in that room. It was truly awesome.

We decided that the next night we would get together again in a different home. That Saturday evening we met at my friends' apartment. There were only seven of us again, although two of them were different from the night before. This time we began by watching a Christian music video while we fellowshipped. We got to know each other better while we drank coffee and ate sandwiches. At about 9:30 pm we decided that we would begin to pray soon, so we started talking about prayer requests. One man said that he wanted prayer to help him with some important decisions that he had to make in his life.

A powerful prophetic anointing came over one of the women present. Although this was only the second time that she had met this man she began to give him a detailed word of knowledge about his life and the state of his salvation. As she spoke he began to tremble with conviction and asked, "What should I do?"

She told him to receive Jesus right then as his personal Lord and Savior and to make Christ the master of his life. He jumped to his feet in the center of the room and she stood with him while leading him in a prayer of repentance and salvation. The rest of us stood up and began to walk around the room with our arms in the air, praising the Lord and thanking Him for this miracle. We exalted Jesus, and as they finished their prayer they joined us in worshipping God.

The thing that happened next I find difficult to describe even now. It is like there are not words that are sufficient for the experience. So, I will attempt within the confines of this language to explain it.

As we were standing, praising and worshipping our Lord an electrifying surge of energy coursed through my body. It started at my head and flooded through my whole being and "Bang!" I was on the floor. I lay there shaking and vibrating as wave after wave of an unseen force washed over and over and over me. I was instantly warm, ...and happy, ...and cozy, ...and loved, and sooo fulfilled. I was "yummy all over inside." Inexpressible joy beyond all human comprehension permeated my body and my thoughts as I lay there in the presence of the Most High God.

Time passed as I tarried in that joyous place and I am not sure how much later it was when I began to become more self-aware again. It was then that I became conscious of my mouth as it was bubbling out in a new tongue. I laughed as this unknown and unmeditated language poured out of my inner belly through my lips. I had never spoken in tongues before, and I marveled at this new fluency flowing out of me like an unending river that I could not have stopped if I had tried.

I sat up and looked around me. I was still very light-headed—almost as though I had been drinking alcohol—but it was different. There was no guilt, only joy. There were no bad side effects, but there surely were lots of good side effects. These I will get to presently.

At that moment though, the most interesting thing to me was the fact that everyone else in the room was also on the floor. Whatever force of God that had struck me had knocked them down as well. A few of us were beginning to stir, but one man and one woman were still lying there. The power of the anointing was still visibly "buzzing" through them as God continued to touch them. All I could do was laugh and bubble in this wondrous new tongue as I watched, unable to even stand. The meeting did not end that night until well after 4:00 am and that was way too soon for all of us.

That was the night that I got FILLED, FILLED, FILLED with the Holy Spirit! I was filled to over-flowing and nothing has ever been the same since!

That week I laid my hands on sick people and they got healed in the Name of Jesus. I shared Jesus with people for the first time with boldness, and they received Him immediately. I cast out demons by the power of Jesus' Name. Within two weeks I was asked to speak at a women's confer-ence, and there were more salvations. God was moving in my life and He was receiving the glory for every miracle. None of it was by my power or might. It was all by the Holy Spirit. He just hap-pened to use me. Glory to God!

You see, I am an ordinary person. I have an ordi-nary life, and ordinary concerns, but my God is EXTRAORDINARY! I did not do anything special after being filled except that I said "Yes Lord," to Him. I let Him use me the way that He wanted to, and I have loved Him with all of my heart and soul and mind.

God is not looking for a perfect vessel in which to move. If He were, He would not be able to use anyone. He is just looking for a willing vessel. He is looking for an ordinary, willing vessel. There are only a few television evangelists and radio talk-show hosts. Thank the Lord for His anointed, but God uses quite a few ordinary folk as well to get the work done for the kingdom.

Are you willing to be an ordinary vessel used by an extraordinary God? Do you want to know how you, too, can be filled to overflowing by the Holy Spirit? If you answered "Yes," to these questions, then read on. In the next chapter I am going to share with you how you, too, can be initially filled by the Holy Ghost, how you can stay filled, and how to walk in the Spirit everyday. This is your day to begin to walk in a new victorious life—filled with the Holy Spirit, empowered for more abundant life and displaying an awesome amount of good, juicy fruit!

THREE

Let There Be Fruit

*W*hen the Holy Spirit came and transformed me it became evident in several ways. Suddenly I was set free from many major sin bondages. I no longer suffered from loneliness, anxiety, greed or lust and I began to easily lead others to Christ. Serving Jesus was no longer difficult, either. I more naturally chose to do the right thing and I had the fortitude to stick to it without much inner turmoil.

I continued to rejoice when I saw a manifestation of God's power, but I now understood to seek the giver and not the gift. I realized that the signs and wonders were to glorify Him who is magnified above all else. The gifts were not for my own personal enjoyment. In fact, I have found that to whom much is given much is also required, but even that has not been a burden. It is pure joy to serve Him in any way that He requires of me. I have been used by Him to heal the sick, cast out demons and even clean the occasional toilet as well.

There is much debate over the value and the use of the gifts, but there is another important aspect to the Holy Spirit that should make every believer hungry for more of Him: good fruit.

This is not just any fruit. This is the choicest, tastiest, brightest fruit that should be found in the life of every Christian. The brightest apple in the pile stands out in front of the others. The most delicious mango can be smelled from across the room. Ripe strawberries make our mouth salivate. Dark red cherries are pleasing to the eye, and there is nothing like a cold juicy piece of watermelon on a hot day. We do not even care what our faces look like as we greedily devour it. It is pleasant for our own consumption and delectable to the taste buds of others, as well.

The fruit of the Spirit draws the unsaved to the believer just like children are drawn to sweet seedless grapes. The fruit of the Spirit is never debated. It is welcomed everywhere. Out of the abundance of this ripe, mature fruit, a delicious spring bursts forth, spilling juice into and onto the lives of everyone we meet.

But the fruit of the Spirit is love, joy, peace, longsuffering, kindness, goodness, faithfulness, gentleness, self-control. Against such there is no law.
- Galatians 5:22-23

The heathen may not believe in miracles and may think that people who speak in tongues are weird, but show them some real unconditional love and they will want to know what makes you tick. Unbelievers love to spend time with Christians who exemplify joy in the middle of trials and tribulations. They may not understand patience, but they do respect it in others.

Good fruit is tasty, and many are drawn to the tree to eat of it. Bad fruit can also be easily seen (and even smelled) some distance away. Jesus told us how to tell what His people really look like. We are not to judge others but we can inspect their fruit. If there is good fruit on the tree, then it is a tree of His. If there is no fruit of the Spirit hanging on it, the tree does not belong to Him.

"Beware of false prophets, who come to you in sheep's clothing, but inwardly they are ravenous wolves. You will know them by their fruits. Do men gather grapes from thornbushes or figs from thistles? Even so, every good tree bears good fruit, but a bad tree bears bad fruit. A good tree cannot bear bad fruit, nor can a bad tree bear good fruit.

- Matthew 7:15-18

Good fruit is important in the life of every person who follows Christ. Without the good juicy fruit of the Holy Spirit how can the world know that we are different? Why would they want what we've got if it is not better than what they have already?

We need to display ripe, tasty, mouth-watering fruit, so that others will want to have some. If we are going to manifest a lot of delicious fruit then we'd better know where to get it. We have got to plug into our source of living water so we can be like a well-watered tree even in the midst of drought. We'd better know what the life-giving source is, and we had better be willing to do whatever it takes to get filled up with it.

The source of this life-giving, empowering fruit is the Holy Spirit. This is why it is called the "Fruit of the Spirit." It comes from the Holy Spirit and it all comes at once. The word is 'fruit' - singular, and not 'fruits' - plural. They manifest all at the same time if their source is the Holy Spirit. One fruit. One believer. All together. This will manifest differently in each person based on their own personality and talents, however, there will definitely be a visible increase in every area.

There is only one way to exhibit love, joy, peace, longsuffering, kindness, goodness, faithfulness, gentleness and self-control all at the same time. This fruit is the result of being filled to overflowing with the Holy Spirit and continuing to be filled with the Holy Spirit. We cannot manifest all nine of these things in our lives at the same time without the ongoing indwelling of the Holy Ghost.

This is the fruit that lets us know that we are indeed filled to overflowing. They cannot be faked all at once. It would be like trying to balance plates on straws while juggling turkeys. A person may seem to exhibit these things for a short period of time, but unless they are truly filled with the Holy Ghost (and continue to be filled), the lies will fall down around them like a house of cards. They may not start out with a sin so obvious as adultery or murder, but they will give in to a more subtle temptation like an outbreak of wrath or selfish ambition. Unless a person is walking out a Spirit-filled life, it is too easy to slide into the desires of the flesh and be ruled by them.

Frequently I come across a blessed saint who tells me that they are filled with the Spirit. When I ask them, "How do you know that you are filled with the Spirit?" there is often a very long pause.

Their inward struggle is apparent on their face as they answer, "Well, I speak in tongues."

"That's fantastic," I respond. "So, if you have all of the fruit of the Spirit outwardly active in your life, tell me your testimony."

There are usually more strange looks as they try to put together what I mean.

At this point I share about the fruit of the Spirit and ask more specifically how they have been transformed. It then becomes apparent that there has been very little transformation in their lives. They marvel when I share some of the testimonies of how the Holy Spirit has changed me, and they can see by my bright and shining countenance that I am speaking the truth. The Holy Spirit confirms it in them. Then I share with that person what I am about to share with you.

Receiving the Holy Spirit is very simple. The Holy Spirit is a gift to us from God. We receive that gift when we are born again, and we can receive more infilling by the Holy Ghost by asking for that as well.

"If you then, being evil, know how to give good gifts to your children, how much more will your heavenly Father give the Holy Spirit to those who ask Him!"

- Luke 11:13

In my own life I received the Holy Spirit when I asked to receive Him and was baptized. I know that I received Him because I asked for Him in faith, and God's Word says that when I ask for the Holy Spirit I will get Him. At that point, however, I was not totally transformed. I did not know about being filled or being continually filled, but the Holy Spirit did affect me in some ways in spite of this. For instance, I did develop a conscience that I had never had before. Unfortunately, I chose to ignore His gentle promptings and continued to serve self instead.

There is no pattern set in concrete concerning the order in which one receives the Holy Spirit. Some people get saved and filled with the Holy Spirit all at once and immediately transform before our eyes.

Others receive Jesus and the Holy Ghost at the same time but do not give up authority to Jesus to baptize them or infill them with the Holy Spirit. They may languish in this unproductive state for years, bearing very little good fruit. However, God wants to pour out more of His Spirit on us. There are two Biblical representations of how He does this. Firstly, as soon as we are willing to yield to His plan, He has provided a simple method for infilling through the laying on of hands.

Now when the apostles who were at Jerusalem heard that Samaria had received the word of God, they sent Peter and John to them, who, when they had come down, prayed for them that they might receive the Holy Spirit. For as yet He had fallen upon none of them. They had only been baptized in the name of the Lord Jesus. Then they laid hands on them, and they received the Holy Spirit.

- Acts 8:14-17

The second Scriptural example of the infilling of the Holy Spirit took place on the Day of Pentecost. God loves variety. When I was filled with the Holy Ghost nobody actually laid hands on me. It was more of a Pentecost experience as the Holy Spirit fell on all of us in the room. Later I realized that He had powerfully impacted and transformed each of us, albeit in very different ways. Another lady and myself were given varying gifts of discernment. A gentleman who was there began to immediately grow in the gift of prophecy, while that has taken much time to develop in me... and I still do not have his sense of revelation. There have been other gift-ings—of hospitality, administrations, and helps—that took many years to slowly develop as I contin-ued to be obedient to the Holy Spirit and come into His presence in that place of continual overflow.

The fruit of the Spirit also began to immediately grow on my Spirit-filled tree. Some were more evi-dent than others, but the transformation was tak-ing place in several important areas.

Once I received the Holy Spirit and was filled up to overflowing, I then had the responsibility of maintaining a full cup. I did not just swallow the ultimate pill to cure all of my ailments, never to take another dose for the rest of my life. I had received and been filled with the great and glorious gift of the Holy Spirit. I needed to be continually filled so that I could experience all of the fruit of the Spirit and glorify God through my changed behavior.

No matter what experience we have when we receive and are filled with the Holy Spirit, we can-not let the process stop there. God has so much more for us, and we will miss it if we think we have it all already. We need to yield to Him totally, and come hungrily before Him asking for more. We need to foster an appetite for the Holy Ghost, while coming thirstily into the presence of the Most High God and seeking Him with all of our hearts.

Our Lord does not want to give us just "a little drop to do us." He wants to pour, pour, and POUR out His Spirit upon us again and again, so that we will have a continual overflow.

And do not be drunk with wine, in which is dissipation; but be filled with the Spirit...

- Ephesians 5:18

In Greek, the tense of the verb "be filled" clearly demonstrates that this is an ongoing process. Even the next words in this segment of Scripture illustrate that this is a continual filling. They give us some helpful tips on how to achieve continual outpour.

...speaking to one another in psalms and hymns and spiritual songs, singing and making melody in your heart to the Lord, giving thanks always for all things to God the Father in the name of our Lord Jesus Christ, submitting to one another in the fear of God.

- Ephesians 5:19-21

Speaking to one another in psalms and hymns and spiritual songs show us an aspect of fellowship with other believers. This kind of fellowship involves the presence and the partnership of the Holy Spirit. There is unity in this kind of gathering, and the Lord loves unity. In the early chapters of Acts when there was an incredible display of the power of the Holy Ghost there was also a common theme of unity. The words "gathered together," "in one accord," and "in unity" are used often. Unity is an attitude that the Holy Spirit desires, and He is drawn to it.

Also, whenever we gather together speaking psalms and singing spiritual songs unto the Lord we are cultivating an appetite for more of the Holy Spirit. Many of these songs will actually invite the Holy Ghost to come and fill us. Our hearts are turned to worship and our humility brings us closer to God.

Singing and making melody in our hearts to the Lord can happen in a group, but it is usually a habit that is fostered in the spiritual life of an individual. When I have been spending a lot of time in the presence of the Holy Spirit there is literally a song playing in my heart. It does not matter if I am alone or in a crowd. Occasionally it even gushes forth, causing me to sing wherever I may be at the time. It may be the words of a familiar hymn, it may be a new song or it may even be in my own prayer language.

Giving thanks always for all things promotes an attitude of thankfulness in every situation. When we are thankful for what we already have God is pleased to increase our portion of blessing. When we are thankful in the midst of trials we show a maturity in spiritual matters and a faith that our Lord loves to reward. When we give thanks for the presence of the Holy Ghost He wants to come and stay and fill us more and more. When we thank Him for the power that is displayed through healings and miracles it glorifies God and shows Him that we realize that it is all Him and not us who accomplishes these signs and wonders.

Submitting to one another is one of the most difficult things that God requires of the believer. In our homes we need to humbly put the needs of others before our own needs. It is by this example that our children will learn and our homes will exemplify peace.

Submission encourages the presence of the Holy Ghost. He is welcome in a home where the wants of others come before the god of self. The "me-me-me" syndrome has been purged from such a place. However, if one member of the family continually puts their personal desires before the needs of the other members, peace is disrupted in the household. They have become their own idol, and they force every other person in that home to bow down and worship them as they rail to get their way. The Holy Spirit will not reside in a home, nor make His manifest presence felt amongst idol worship, pride and rebellion to the Word of God. We need to lay self down and be filled with the Holy Spirit.

Fellowshipping with believers, worshiping and submission are just a few of the things that encourage the presence of the Holy Spirit. When I was filled with the Holy Spirit it did not end there—it was just beginning. After that day I gained an insatiable appetite for the things of God that has never gone away, because I immediately began to feed it. Later that week I went to two awesome Holy Ghost meetings and sat right on the front row soaking up everything that I could get from God. I was hungry and I cried out to Him for more!

God is wonderful! He continued to fill me with His Holy Spirit. Over those next weeks I was delivered of so much bondage and set free from so many overwhelming habits of sin that I have since lost count. I am free! I have victory in my day-to-day life that was not there before and cannot be denied now. People are blown away by the fruit of the Spirit that gushes forth from me and it causes them to be changed as well. Glory to God!

Over the next few years the Lord has faithfully shown me how to keep that cup overflowing with His goodness. There has never been a drought as I have learned to feed my spirit on the things of God. I praise His mighty Name and marvel at all that He has done for me.

The good news is that He has done these things for you as well. In Jesus' Name you, too, can walk in the glorious path of victory and be set free from all that binds you. I encourage you to read on and see how God has changed the life of this ordinary believer and how He can give you freedom from worry, healing and restoration, peace and joy even in the middle of trials and tribulations. We serve a miracle-making God who can transform you and your situation. May you be greatly blessed by His presence as you continue to read, and may He continually fill you with His amazing Holy Spirit of grace and power. In the Name of Jesus I pray this over you.

Amen.

FOUR

The Power Of Love

*L*ove is a powerful force that links all of mankind. While not everyone feels that they have been loved, most people understand what it means to love another person. Love is a wonderful emotion that allows us to extend beyond ourselves for the sake of the one that we care for. Many parents love their children and would give up their own comfort, or even their own lives, for their little ones. Romantic love has motivated conquerors to conquer. Steadfast love causes families to stay together. Brotherly love (although much out of style), has in the past built family dynasties.

All love, however, is not necessarily good, and not all love is inspired by the Holy Ghost. Self- love, for instance, can destroy a marriage. It is also the substance that an abusive individual thrives on. This love for one's own desires overrides the need to one's own children. Feeding self-love and selfishness in an unstable person can eventually motivate them to steal, rape, murder or even torture for their twisted sense of pleasure.

Everyone knows what it feels like to love themselves or someone else. Jesus said, "But if you love those who love you, what credit is that to you? For even sinners love those who love them" (Luke 6:32).

Even sinners love those who love them. There is a whole world of sinners who love those who love them, but care very little for those that they do not know. This is how everyone can know about love, while we have so much hate and racism around us. We flash romantic love across our television screens 24 hours a day, seven days a week, and yet divorce abounds. Our culture tells us that we should only be in love with someone who acts like they are plain crazy about us. They put little value on loving unconditionally in a steadfast manner. When we love only those who love us (or even worse, those who act like they love us), this is a very shallow kind of love that will never impact anyone to change. This is not the kind of love that Jesus loved with.

Jesus loved us with all that He had. He laid down His own life for us. He loved us enough to die for us. This is the kind of love that impacts the world. Many historians who are not even Christians will recognize Jesus as being the one person who has done the most for humanity. If they do not believe that He died for them, what is it that they think that

He did that was so great? They will point to His teachings–the teachings of love.

This is the kind of love that will make a difference. It is the kind of love that can change our own personal situation as well.

Holy Ghost love is powerful and anointed to love the unlovable. Several years ago, when I was still walking around with one and a half feet still in the world, the Lord brought a very special lady into my life. She was the first real female friend I had ever had. I did not choose her. In fact, I would not have done that. It was the nature of my sin to only involve myself with men. I thought that women were too competitive, but in truth, I was too competitive. I found women to be too judgmental, but in retrospect I understand now why they were. After all, I dressed to get men's attention, and I behaved shamefully.

At the time I was a single mother of a sweet baby boy. I had recently come out of a women's shelter and was trying desperately to gain some order and security in my life. Into the middle of this chaos the Lord brought Gloria.

Gloria was everything that I was not. She was happily married, living in a nice home and secure with her husband and their three children. She was very busy with family, church activities and hobbies, yet she always had time for those around her that needed a little extra. I needed a lot extra.

I wonder if she knew what she was getting involved in when she befriended me. I know now, though, that it was the Holy Spirit coursing through her that gave her the strength and the wisdom that she needed.

As I was new to her city, Gloria insisted that I take an apartment half a block from her house so that I would be close enough to borrow toilet paper if I needed it. Her house was always open to me if I wanted a cup of tea. I could call her anytime of day or night with an emergency. She was there when my babysitter fell through. She drove me to Bible studies and to church in bad weather. She had me over for supper when my cupboards were bare (which was sometimes three times a week). She talked to me for hours about any and every subject that I needed to discuss.

Even with all of the time and energy that she spent on me, Gloria was an incredible mother to her children. This, too, was a tremendous example to me. With all of the activities, clubs and sports that come with running a home full of children, she never wore a frustrated look. I watched her eldest daughter go through her teenage years without uttering a nasty word to her mother. The children helped out in that home as though that was all they were born to do. There was love, joy, peace and harmony in that house. The Holy Spirit was welcome there, and so was I. The way that she made me feel was remarkable to me. It was like I was her very best friend in the whole world. It took me years to realize that she had that same kind of friendship with several women. She also had an especially deep relationship with her husband. Most of all, however, she had an incredible closeness with the Holy Spirit.

Gloria taught me friendship by being my friend. She taught me how to love the unlovable by loving me. She taught me how to love someone who is still trying to serve two masters without compromising her own values.

I will never forget the conversation that we had after two years of friendship. In the doorway of her home, Gloria had taken me by the hand and was looking into my eyes. Then she apologized to me for not being a good enough friend to confront the sin in my life. She felt that she had not been there enough for me to come to, or that possibly she had not been strong enough to discuss those things. She thought that she had let me down.

Through many tears and much confession I poured out the mess I had been making of my life. I was ashamed of my actions, but I was even more ashamed that this blessed woman of God felt somehow responsible. It was my sin, not hers. She had done nothing wrong. It had probably made her uncomfortable every time I came around, but she had loved me anyway. It was by her love for me that she had earned the right to correct me. Her rebuke was gentle, but firm. It stung, and conviction rushed upon me like a mighty waterfall.

It was not long after that I bowed my knee to Jesus and gave Him everything.

I learned to love a friend by having a friend in Gloria. I loved her then. I love her still.

She moved over a thousand miles away. I often think of her, although I have not called nor written nearly enough. Over the years the seeds that she planted in me have grown to maturity. I mother my children in many of the ways that I have seen her do. I have cultivated my own friendship with Jesus that gives me the security that I so desperately need. I also have many female friends now, and it often amazes me when one of them refers to me as their "best friend."

We often talk about there being no greater love than to lay our lives down for another. As Christians we talk about dying for Jesus and how we ought to be willing to do this. Dying for Jesus however, is a quick, one-second decision in the face of an immediate danger. Living for Jesus everyday is quite another matter.

Living for Jesus means loving for Jesus. It is not the same as the world's idea of "I will love you if you love me." There are no conditions on the love of Jesus. We need to love the unlovable. We need to reach out to the unreachable long before they know to reach for us. We need to love when we are not received. We need to love when we do not see a difference. We need to love when it is not convenient, and when we have loved enough to earn the right, we need to give a rebuke in love, even when we may face rejection as a result.

And let us not grow weary while doing good, for in due season we shall reap if we do not lose heart.

- Galatians 6:9

When I became filled with the Holy Spirit I passed over the bridge from being the one receiving love to being someone who is giving love. An exciting side effect is how this changed my ability to share the gospel. Before I was filled with the Holy Spirit my testimony was weak and tainted by my sin, but once I was filled with the Holy Spirit, the transformation in me was apparent to all who knew me. I had been changed. There was no denying it. I radiated joy and gushed with power and boldness. I had an immediate gifting of discernment (knowing when to speak and when to be quiet). But more than any of these, I had love, love, love!

Three years of seething and loathing for my estranged husband was washed away. I was finally able to forgive. All of the hatred was gone. I was free!

Other stressed relationships also began to heal. I was free!

Free people set other people free.

I was suddenly keenly aware that if I did not share the gospel with an individual that he or she would go to hell. I was emotionally involved with the hurting and the lost. I could feel their pain and I loved them. I could not help myself.

When you love somebody you want the best for him or her. The good news about Jesus Christ is the best news that any person can receive. I love to share the gospel because I love Jesus and I love those that He loves. I could not stop sharing the gospel if I tried.

Preachers sometimes wonder, "How do I get people to evangelize?"

Stop wondering, and encourage them to be filled with the Holy Spirit! Out of an overflowing cup we have all that we need to minister to others. Only when we are filled to overflowing do we have an outpouring of love that cannot be stopped by "unlovability".

Love is a phenomenal tool when it is placed in the hands of a Spirit-filled believer. When a man comes to you and says, "My kids don't like your Sunday school program and your sermons are too long," love allows you to see right past that into the heart of the matter. With love and a Holy Ghost anointing you can reply, "Brother, if you feel called by God to join XYZ Church, then you pray about it and do as He leads you. We love you and will pray for you regardless of where you attend."

When your neighbor comes screaming at you from across the fence uttering threats and obscenities you will respond, "Neighbor, I forgive you. Jesus loves you, and you just made my prayer list!"

By the way, if you actually do put them on your prayer list, you will both benefit from that as well. There was an acquaintance of mine that I did not know that well who took it upon himself to spend much time spreading poisonous lies and gossip about me wherever idle ears would stop and listen. When I found out about the situation I began to pray, seeking the Lord's guidance. I felt the Holy Spirit continually reminding me not to try to validate either myself or my ministry to this person or to those that he sought to corrupt. I was encouraged by my Lord not to seek retaliation in any way. Instead, my ever present Counselor led me to pray for this man.

For the first two months I prayed for him once a week. Then I met him one day on the street, and he deliberately avoided making eye contact. I then increased my prayers for him to twice a week. Again, I met him downtown and was virtually snubbed. Undaunted, I went to three and then four prayer spots per week for him and his family.

Prayer for this individual has become a regular exercise for me and I have even come to enjoy it. I praise the Lord for him. I ask for his salvation and a sudden complete transformation that will be a sign and a wonder to many. I pray the Scriptures over him and his family asking for unity and love to abound in his household.

One day I almost ran face first into this man in the post office. My own response was most amazing. Before I even had time to think about what I was doing, I was happily greeting him like he was my long lost buddy. He was blown over by the love in my voice and chatted to me pleasantly for several minutes before continuing on his way.

When I returned home later that day I prayed about what had happened. I discovered that through my prayers God was giving me a deep love for this person. When I was faced with his presence I couldn't help but to show it.

I do not know if this person feels any differently about me. It does not matter. I will continue to pray for him and his family even if they openly persecute me. It is not my responsibility to change them—it is my responsibility to pray for them and love them just like Jesus loved me when I did not deserve it. I thank Him just about everyday that He did not let my behavior effect His love for me.

Holy Spirit love is not the natural love of loving those who openly love you. It is unnatural to love those who hurt you. However, when we are filled to overflowing with the Holy Spirit, we are anointed to love people the way that Jesus loves them. This is the kind of love that heals the hurting, forgives the unforgivable and loves the unlovable. This is the kind of love that can change the world. It is the kind of love that has been written in stories and remembered for more than 2000 years. This kind of love is good juicy fruit on any tree.

May the Holy Spirit fill you and cause you to display an abundance of love even to those who are unlovable. May He fill your cup, with more of Himself so that you will have lots of overflow to share the love of Jesus to those around you more effectively. In Jesus' name I pray.

Amen.

FIVE

Holy Ghost Joy

When I walk down the street and I pass by somebody that I know, I always cheerfully ask them, "How are you today?"

The world has several answers to that question and most of them could only be described as purely miserable. Some answer "Fine," but they do not even look that well. Another will give me a response based on the weather.

"I'd be a lot better if the sun was shining," they say.

Frequently, however, I will run into someone who will give me a list of ailments longer than my right arm, making me sorry that I asked.

After answering me in a worn-out monotone voice, they will often ask me the same question.

"Awesome!!!" I respond jubilantly. Their eyes come open as though they have just been bit, and they take a step backwards. My joy has startled them speechless and they may take a moment to recover. At that point I usually add, "If I felt any better I would break into song!" They may at that moment take a wide step around me, as though they are anxious to get away from me. Occasionally, though, they stop dead in their tracks and ask me why I am so happy.

Many times I have shared Jesus with a person at a time like that. They can see that I have something that they do not have and they want it. So I share with them that it is not a something, it is a someone. Jesus is in me, and I cannot help but be joyous. The Holy Ghost is coursing through my veins and greater is He who is in me, than he who is in the world!

As a Christian my life needs to be a living testimony of the light of Christ shining through me. Joy bubbles forth from me on a regular basis. Frequently even in the midst of a trying situation the Lord will show me something funny and I will have a great big belly laugh.

How long has it been since you have had a great big belly laugh? ...a real good hard one that causes your teeth to shake, your belly to jiggle, and makes you snort like a cow!?

Even scientists now agree with the wisdom of God.

 A merry heart does good, like medicine, But a broken spirit dries the bones.

- Proverbs 17:22

I have noticed that a broken spirit dries the face, too! As we age we can look in the mirror to see if we have spent most of our lives smiling or frowning. Frowns take much more effort and crease the face in an unholy manner, leaving behind their tired tracks. Joyous people enjoy fewer lines and what lines they do have all run in an upward direction, causing the person to look jolly and sweet. Those who have spent their life in a scowl wear that scowl in their old age. So, your mother was right when she said, "Don't do that with your face or it will freeze that way!"

Joy is the calling card of the believer. It cannot be faked very long. Anyone can have a few minutes of happiness as they laugh at a joke or satisfy their desires with money or lust, but real joy is happiness that continues.

A person who is continually filled to overflowing with the Holy Spirit will have joy just about non-stop. Now I say "just about", because until we go home to be with the Lord we do live in a body of flesh in the middle of a corrupt world. Injustice may give us a burden to pray, we may feel someone else's sadness as we experience empathy or we may get angry at an intolerable situation. However, we do not hang around in depression, wrath and misery of various sorts.

Before I was washed by the Blood of the Lamb and transformed by the Holy Spirit, I was a nasty individual. I used to enjoy telling people off. I took great pride in how well I could tell someone where to go and how fast to get there. When I got angry at somebody I could hold a grudge for weeks or even years. As a master of misery, I often plotted revenge or fantasized how I would make that person pay for what they had done. When I was depressed, I was very good at it. I could cry for half the night, wake up with puffy eyes and bawl some more by lunch. I could go on and on about the evils of this world and all of the people who hurt me.

If you came over to my house during one of my pity parties you also would have been contaminated by my misery. We would have spent time in idle chatter and gossiping about every person that came to mind. It is catching. "Birds of a feather flock together," my Grandmother use to say. When it comes to unhappiness this is definitely true.

If you don't believe this, get filled with the Holy Ghost and go giddy on your friends. A few will get saved and transformed; the rest will get suddenly get sick and not want to come out to play anymore. That's okay. Let them go home and watch you from a distance. Keep on praying for them, and when they see how much fun you are having, it won't take too long before they come cautiously sniffing around again.

Once you have been filled to overflowing with the Holy Spirit, you will have something good to give them. It is called "outpour." Outpour of love. Outpour of joy. Outpour of gentleness and kindness. It just pours out of you in a way that is not offensive. There is no offence in the tasty fruit of the Spirit. The lost are drawn to outpour, because they see answers in it to their dilemmas. They see hope in outpour and they see a person who has been transformed — a person, who used to get down in the muck with them, has risen above the circumstances and there is victory in that transformation. The hurting people of this world need to see more fruit of that nature.

When I was filled to overflowing with the Holy Spirit the fizzle came out of my fight. I began to realize that the things that made me angry were really not mine to bear. They belonged to Jesus.

"Come to Me, all you who labor and are heavy laden, and I will give you rest. Take My yoke upon you and learn from Me, for I am gentle and lowly in heart, and you will find rest for your souls. For my yoke is easy and My burden is light."

- Matthew 11:28-30

Walking around with anger and worry gives us stress. It feels like fifty pounds of rocks are tied to our backs and the weight is tiring. But Jesus wants to take that load for us, and if we belong to Him, we need to let Him have it. If we do not give up the heavy yoke, we are trying to do Jesus' job for Him.

We are playing God. That is a heavy load. Jesus can have my burdens. He wants them. He can have them. I will take up His yoke of love, joy and peace any day.

I have given up my anger and stress to Jesus and I do not intend to pick them up ever again. Before Jesus came and changed me, I was angry twenty days out of the month and depressed the other ten. Now I get real angry a couple of times a year, and depressed maybe once. Even on those occasions, what use to take days or weeks to get rid of is now gone in hours. I cannot even get depressed anymore if I try.

The last time it happened was about six months ago. The devil had attacked our finances and it was looking pretty grim for Christmas. The children were unusually unruly and demanding my attention. I had received three phone calls that morning, two with more bad news, and the other was a bill collector. In the natural, things were looking very bad. My head was spinning with all of the evil developments as I tried to make lunch for the kids. I got short with them several times as they were reacting to my lousy attitude. Finally, my six-year-old son straightened me out.

He came to me at the kitchen table, gave me a big hug and said, "Mom, I think you better go spend some time with the Lord. I think the devil is trying to steal your joy!"

Instantly I began to laugh and even cry a little at the same time. I wiped away my tears with the back of my hand and gave him another squeeze. "You know what, son?" I responded, "I think that you are right," and I marveled at the discernment of my little boy as I went to pray.

I spent some time on my knees that afternoon, and I saturated my spirit with some good preaching tapes as well. By supper time I was completely set free from depression and ready to go to war in the spiritual realm. The good news began to pour in the following morning.

Weeping may endure for a night, But joy comes in the morning.
- Psalm 30:56

Over the next two weeks, we received over $400 in cash and gift certificates. There were also three huge food hampers that were delivered to our door, and hundreds of dollars worth of presents for the children and me. We have never had a more blessed Christmas.

In years past I have gone out and spent much money and time making everything "just so" for the holidays, but last year was the best ever. Jesus bought me things I would never have got for myself. He blessed me with things that I thought too extravagant to spend money on. He delivered every toy that the children desired, and even a few special things that I would not have thought to buy. The food hampers, also, were laden with decadent items I would never have purchased for our table, and there was enough for the next month and a half as well.

God knows how to give good gifts to His children. Praise His Holy Name!

The enemy had tried to harm us but instead we had much rejoicing in the Lord, and long after the food was eaten, our joy lingered on.

> *...the joy of the Lord is your strength.*
> *- Nehemiah 8:10b*

It really is! Joy is a practical tool for a Spirit-filled believer. It gives me strength even when things do not look like they are going well.

We proclaim excellent health over our household and seldom do we suffer with childhood maladies that sweep through our community. When they do find us, we rebuke them quickly in the Name of the Lord so they do not generally hang around very long. However, one cold wintry week last year one got us. For the third night in a row, I shuffled from bed to bed half asleep dispensing medicine, hugs and prayers. My little girl, Naomi (whose name means joy), decided to give out her own special brand of happiness in the darkest hour.

She had been up several times, and in an effort to calm her down I decided to climb into bed beside her. I stroked her hair, comforting her, hoping she would fall asleep so that we all could finally get some rest. As I lay there in the twilight drifting off to dreamland I became remotely aware that she was sitting over the top of my head. My eyes fluttered open as I regained consciousness. I was just in time to see her take her two biggest fingers and JAM THEM UP MY NOSE!

Joy alert!

Not!

Well, there was no use getting angry. She was sleepily gurgling and cooing, oblivious to what she had done, while I was reeling in pain. It took a week for the lining to grow back in my nose, but even though it hurt, it did not take me long to realize how funny it was.

Naomi is a bundle of two-year-old joy; a precious gift given to me by God. Another time, I had just finished putting the children to bed and had turned on some praise music that I like to listen to while I tidy up. As I left the living room on my way to the kitchen, I became aware that I was being followed. I turned around to see Naomi clambering up onto the sofa. When she saw that she had been caught she gave me her biggest grin, and thrust both arms into the air swaying to the music. "Halawuya!" she declared triumphantly.

I stopped and smiled down at her. "Yes, you are very cute," I said. Then through gritted teeth I continued, "Now, get to bed!"

The children are a constant source of joy and encouragement to me. As they are being raised surrounded by joy, it has seeded their souls and it is frequently harvested from the things that they say. I often hear Naomi and my four-year-old, Joshua, singing loudly, "I've got that joy, joy, joy, joy down in my heart!" This is especially pleasing while driving through the city, lost and late for an important appointment.

The joy of the Lord is my strength! Ultimately, it is always God who restores my joy. The Holy Spirit has taught me that nothing replenishes my soul like time spent joyously praising Him. As I worship Him with gladness and thankfulness, joy pours into my very being. When I am not feeling as merry, I bring Him a sacrifice of joy anyway. I work myself up to it, and He blesses me by defeating my circumstances and the enemy as a result.

And now my head shall be lifted up above my enemies all around me; Therefore I will offer sacrifices of joy in His tabernacle; I will sing, yes, I will sing praises to the Lord.

- Psalm 27:6

Joy is the brightest, tastiest part of the fruit of the Spirit. It is the part that is the easiest to see. It glows in the life of the Spirit-filled believer, shining forth as light in the darkness of this world. Joy is the instantaneous response that cannot be bottled up. It is the element that makes us a little radical.

To those who are seeking truth and desiring change, joy will draw them like flies to a hot bug zapper. To those who focus on every letter of the law but care not for the things of the heart, joy is indigestible. They cannot stomach our laughs and do not understand our humor. The things of the darkness have little to do with the things of the light.

Joy is a fruit of the Holy Spirit. We cannot be filled to overflowing and not display a lot of joy in our lives. A Christian who does not exemplify joy may have received the Holy Spirit, but they are certainly not filled to overflowing.

"He who believes in Me, as the Scripture has said, out of his heart [belly KJV] will flow rivers of living water." But this He spoke concerning the Spirit, whom those believing in Him would receive; for the Holy Spirit was not yet given, because Jesus was not yet glorified.

- John 7:38-39

The Holy Spirit flows forth from the belly. Laughter flows forth from the belly. Joy is a fruit of the Holy Ghost. It is a torrent of water that cannot be turned off.

If you are a believer but are not yet experiencing an abundance of joy, do not pray for only more joy.

Pray for more of the Holy Spirit. Pray to be filled to overflowing.

Run—don't walk—down to the wildest Holy Ghost meeting you can find. Sit right on the front row and ask God to fill up your cup until you over- flow. Keep going back until He does.

Continual overflow results from continual filling.

Heavenly Father, I lift up to You the people who are reading this book right now. Lord, I ask You to fill them more and more with Your Holy Spirit. Come upon them right now, and as a result, give them more of Your fruit of joy in their lives. Heal the brokenhearted. Give them the oil of joy for mourning and the garment of praise for the spirit of heaviness. Restore to them lost emotions, and may this trans- formation be bright and pleasing to the eye so that all who they come in contact with them will see that manifest joy pouring forth from their lives.

I ask You, Lord, that there would be such an abundance of laughter that it cannot be contained— that it will bubble over and spill onto the lives of others around them. I ask that that joy would draw others to them and that it would burst from their innermost beings, pressed down, shaken together and overflowing, to the glory of Your Name. In Jesus' Name,

Amen.

SIX

Peace That Transcends All Understanding

World peace is a hot topic these days. Everybody wants to know how we can obtain peace between nations. When will all of the wars stop?

Peace, however cannot be obtained on a global level until it is established on a personal level. People who are peaceful produce peace. Those who war against their own souls can seldom keep peace in their own families, never mind their nation.

The apostle Peter encourages us to live peacefully within ourselves, as well as with those around us.

Beloved, I beg you as sojourners and pilgrims, abstain from fleshly lusts which war against the soul.

- 1 Peter 2:11-12

Fleshly lusts war against our souls. Things that feed our flesh and not our spirit are fleshly lusts. Greed, envy, unholy sexual passions, addictions and gluttony are just a few. They wage war against our soul, making it difficult to function. They color our perspective on life. They cause us to see only how a situation will satisfy our personal needs.

For instance, we see money as a means to get more material things that we want, instead of as a means to bless others or to buy more Christian material to feed our spirit. We store up tonnes of food in our own pantries instead of giving some away to the needy. We smoke, we drink alcohol, and haughtily dismiss any idea that it is not good for our body, nor do we give any thought to how many Bibles could be bought with the money we spent on our avarice. We call our sexual desires a lifestyle instead of sin, but in the middle of it all we have no peace. That is key. If there is no peace, and it is such a struggle to justify even to ourselves when we look in the mirror, then something must be wrong.

It is wrong. It is a sin that feeds the flesh and wages war on our own soul. This is why there is so much guilt, so much misery and so much dissatisfaction. That is why there is a constant striving for more to fill the void. More money, more sex, more alcohol, …and just one cigarette is never enough to calm the stress. That is because the cigarette is causing the stress. It is not building the soul—it is waging a war against it. One is never enough.

Before I was filled with the Holy Spirit, I looked at everything through the eyes of fleshly lust. I had a huge, endless void in my life that I tried to fill with every kind of unholy substance, and the void only seemed to get bigger and bigger. Whatever my tongue desired, the rest of my body was forced to deal with. I only worked at what I could make the most money doing. I was not interested in helping anyone do anything for free. I smoked and drank alcohol as my flesh ruled my life. I fostered sexual fantasy in my mind.

Are you shocked? You should not be. I have no doubt that you have done some of these things too, and probably a few others I did not mention.

Sin abounds in this world. It is everywhere. That is why I know, that I know, that I know, that I have Somebody great by having the Holy Spirit in my life. Sin definitely ruled me before I had the Holy Spirit. If I could have gotten rid of it on my own, I would have. If I could have fixed the problem by seeing a psychiatrist, I would have kept going to one. If the world had an answer to the war that rages in the souls of mankind they would bottle it and sell it. It cannot be bought, but it can be received.

The answer is the fruit of the Spirit. It comes by being filled with the Spirit.

It is peace. Peace of mind. It is the peace that transcends all understanding.

Be anxious for nothing, but in everything by prayer and supplication, with thanksgiving, let your requests be made known to God; and the peace of God, which surpasses all understanding, will guard your hearts and minds through Christ Jesus.

- Philippians 4:6

When I became filled with the Holy Spirit the Lord planted a seed in me that began to produce good fruit. It was wonderful.

At night, for the first time in my life, I began to enjoy a phenomenal peace. I would (and still do) love to lie in my bed chatting with the Holy Spirit before I would drift off into blessed sleep. I would praise Him, and thank Him, and tell Him that I loved Him. I would briefly discuss the day's events with Him. I would think things through as I felt Him direct me to His Word and His thoughts. I would make my requests known to Him.

Afterwards there would be this amazing peace. There was this happiness without worry that would fizz there inside of me. I could physically feel it, kind of in my heart and beside my heart and in my belly. A warm glowing joy would envelope me, and I would fall soundly into a carefree sleep.

Every night I am still amazed as this phenomenal peace washes over me. The Holy Spirit is often the last one that I talk to and the last one that I think of before I drift off into peaceful slumberland.

Three weeks after my transformation I woke up one morning and blissfully stretched. As I lay there on my bed, basking in the comfort of the lingering presence of the Holy Ghost, I began to think. The events of the previous weeks had been a whirlwind of activity, with major changes and decisions flung at me daily. Yet, I was at total peace. Nothing had rocked my boat even once.

I also realized that there had been other unexpected side-effects to being completely filled with the Holy Spirit. I was no longer swearing. I used to curse, even in my thoughts, but I could not even remember the last foul word that had come to my mind or escaped my lips. There were also no more filthy dreams. They had completely stopped. No more nightmares, either. Not only that, but there was now an aversion to perversion. I had been plagued with various unholy sexual temptations, and my eyes used to be drawn to any spectacle on television or on the city street. Now it caused me to feel revulsion in my stomach. I was instantly aware of the sin and burdened to pray about it.

Over the years since then I have often been asked about feeling lonely. Many people experience loneliness whether they are married or single. I used to be lonely when I was married and I was lonely during my single life. However, when I was filled with the Holy Spirit all loneliness fled. I have not experienced that emotion since. I was transformed by the wonderful filling and indwelling of the Holy Ghost. Praise the Lord!

I encourage you, whether you burn with sexual lust or suffer from loneliness, get filled up with the Holy Spirit. Stop looking for a person to meet those needs. Make Jesus your number one priority and spend time in the empowering presence of the Spirit. It will make a world of difference as you continue to be filled. Once you make the Holy Spirit your new lifestyle, He will set you free and fill every void in your life in a way that no person will ever be able to satisfy.

The void that we experience is there because God put it there so we would seek Him out to fill it. We are incomplete until we face that fact and choose to fill that spot with more of Him. That is why no earthly relationship ever meets the need. Nobody is able to measure up.

Even when we immerse ourselves in a romance, it eventually wears out. In fact, putting a person in that place where God is supposed to be makes that person the object of our worship. That person that we love and treasure more highly than our relationship with our Lord becomes an idol in our life. It is little wonder that those intensely passionate beginnings become stale later on.

When we do not put Jesus first in our lives we lack His blessings even on our love, because if we do not worship Him over all else we have made something else our god. Our Lord is yearning for that place of priority in our lives. When we submit ourselves to being overfilled with His Spirit, He is in that place of ongoing worship where He ought to be. We then become blessed with abundant fruit as He pours out in us.

In our "throw away" society we eat things up and throw out the wrappers. We buy nice things and pass on our leftovers. We use up spouses and then find a newer, younger model. None of these things bring lasting peace, though. Only the Holy Spirit can do that.

We may think we are happy doing things our own way. We may think that we are having a good time enjoying our cigarettes, our beer or our little bit of "harmless" gossip. Are we, though?

When we go to bed each night do we experience that peace which surpasses all understanding? Real peace is another fruit that cannot be faked for very long. We may look cool to people who do not know us well, but our family knows if peace reigns in our heart. Continual outbursts of anger show a lack of peace. Worry over money shows a lack of peace. Overwhelming desires for sex, money or food that involve a lot of preliminary fantasizing or planning suggest a real lack of peace.

We do not need more money, more help or more sleep to get peace. We need more of the Holy Spirit.

I used to have so much worry. I was always striving to make more money; but the more I made, the more I needed. When the Holy Ghost got involved, He taught me things about finances that I needed to know. He directed me to sow into the kingdom of God, and He led me through the Scriptures to educate me about wealth. I learned to tithe and trust Him. I learned to give and believe God for increase. I learned to help out whenever I could without expecting pay.

The Holy Spirit has taught me that I belong to God. When He showed me how to tithe I did not argue with Him. I did not tell Him, "That is only in the Old Testament law." (I am very glad that I did not, now that I know that it preceded the law.) I did not whine to God, "How will I ever make it without that money?" Instead, I listened to Him and believed that He would rebuke the devourer for my sake.

And He does. I do not ever have to work myself into a sweat over it. I just let my requests be made known to God and then I have peace. He has the job of filling the need. I have the job of being continually filled by Him. This makes faith easy.

It works really well. Only three weeks ago, my dryer broke down. I have three small children, and this presented a problem. I did not, however, allow fear to rise up in me. I took my clothes to the laundromat to dry them and did not worry about it.

That night I laid my request before Him and believed in faith that He is my supplier. Then I forgot about it for a couple of days. On the next Saturday afternoon I took another pile of clothes to the laundromat. While I was there, I chatted with a neighbor about my broken down-down dryer. He told me that he did not have a washer and that he had no plans to buy one. As a single man who worked all week, he enjoyed using the public facility, but he did have a working dryer that he did not use...

I asked him how much he would like for it, and he gave it to me for free. He and his friend delivered it later that day and even set it up for me. Praise God!

That morning, before I had left the house, a lady had delivered a slightly used $2000 vacuum cleaner as well. These were not just by chance. The Lord had heard my prayers and was faithful to look after us. Glory to His Holy Name!

I have peace because I belong to Jesus. I can call on Him for normal, everyday needs and be confident that He cares for me and will supply. Seldom do I ever lose any peace. Perhaps once a year I do experience a bit of heavy stress as I give into my flesh in a weak moment of crisis. However, God has built a contingency plan into my life for those occasions.

One day, early last winter, I did forget my peace at home during a shopping trip to a nearby town. Fortunately, though, my children remembered to bring theirs with them. We were thirty miles from home in our next-to-new van. Hearing a little beep, I looked down to see that the engine light had come on.

The devil was right there to remind me that we were 46 miles over the warranty. I quickly made a detour in our plans and pulled into the nearby dealership parking lot. I was already tallying up the financial damages in my head. There was that nasty pressure in my gut as I was giving way to evil anxiety.

The children had noticed that we had left our usual migrating path and began to pummel me with questions. As we pulled into a parking spot, I told them to hush while making harsh, pained expressions. As we came to a stop my eldest, Zechariah, moved to the front seat and asked me what was wrong.

I explained the situation, being as calm as I could, but expressed that we might be there for a while. We would have to wait to find a ride home again, and our afternoon plans would likely have to be cancelled. I will never forget the look on Zechariah's face as he turned to face me solidly. "Mom," he asked, "where is your faith?"

My mouth dropped open as he continued. "You know that God always looks after us. He will figure this out too, and it won't cost us a cent."

Out of the mouth of babes!

His rebuke straightened me right out. We put our heads down together and committed the whole thing to the Lord. God's peace washed over me, and I knew that it was going to be all right.

Zechariah was right. God did look after us. We drove away from there within fifteen minutes, and it had not cost us a cent. It had been a small problem. A mechanic who had stayed later than usual volunteered to look at it even though he should have been home eating his supper. He fixed it quickly and did not even charge us. We drove away, praising the Lord and glorifying His holy Name! Later that night I marveled at the peace and faith that God had given my little boy.

Jesus loves us and He does look after us. He will do the same for you as well. You do not need more money—you need more of Him.

People in the world say that they want peace. But at the same time they want to keep their anger, their sin, their rebellion, their foolishness and every bad habit that money can buy. These things wage war against their own souls and make peace impossible in their homes. Without peace in their own homes, how can they know how to bring peace to the world? If we are not peace-makers at home we will not have that blessing in the world either. If we really want world peace, we need to pray for peace in individuals first. We need to pray that world leaders get filled with the Holy Ghost so peace will flow out of their lives.

Being filled with the Holy Spirit is what gives us real peace. It is a fruit that can be shared, as well, and it tastes good to those who eat it.

The juicy fruit of peace is another powerful tool in the equipment bag of a salvation-minded, Spirit-filled believer.

A few years ago when I was in a women's shelter I was surrounded by a lot of unrest. The women there had been emotionally and often physically abused. The children also visibly suffered from the effects of dysfunctional homes. Many of them were on Ritallin and the stress level was very high. A group of us ladies were having a talk about the situations that we had left behind. Several of us bared our souls to one another that afternoon while we sat in a sunlit backyard over coffees. One of the women who had not said too much suddenly spoke up, "Why do you seem so different from the rest of us? If I had gone through what you went through I don't think that I could laugh about it."

I smiled at her and looked deep into her eyes as I replied, "It is because I have Jesus in me, and He has the power to calm the storm, or calm me in the midst of the storm."

There was a quiet that settled over each of them for a long moment. Then one gal beside me said softly, "I don't know what that is, but I sure want it." Two days later, she gave her life to Jesus Christ.

Peace is a tool that impacts people for the gospel. It can be seen on the mature tree of a believer who is full to overflowing with the Holy Spirit.

Having peace does not mean that everything always goes perfectly for us without any challenges. It just means that the storms of life will not break us up. We will bend like a tree in the wind, but we will continue to bear good fruit year after year.

I pray that you will enjoy the delicious fruit of peace in your life today. As you read, may the Holy Spirit continue to fill you up and overflow peace onto those around you. May you exemplify peace, and may you be a peace-maker wherever you go.

Most of all, I pray that you will be filled, filled, filled, with the Holy Spirit. Out of your relationship with Him, you will be abundantly blessed with more peace than you had ever thought possible. In Jesus' Name I pray.

Amen.

SEVEN

Longsuffering

A few years ago, I heard a preacher talking about patience. He made the point that it is something that a believer should never pray to receive more of. He said that when we pray for patience God might answer that prayer by pouring out trials and tribulations to make us stronger and therefore more patient. He was referring to this Scripture:

My brethren, count it all joy when you fall into various trials, knowing that the testing of your faith produces patience.
- James 1:2

We have heard that patience is a virtue, but it is also a fruit of the Holy Spirit. In reality then, we do not have to pray for more patience. All we have to do is be continually filled with the Holy Ghost and the fruit of longsuffering will abundantly grow on our tree.

In the western hemisphere we do not like to use the word longsuffering. It conjures up nasty images of physical pain and martyrdom that we have difficulty relating to. In some parts of the world, however, that aspect of longsuffering is commonly put to use in the day-to-day sacrifices of believers. Even when jailed and tortured, they continue to bear the light of Christ before the very people who persecute them. They are empowered by the Holy Spirit to be more burdened for the souls around them than for their own bodies. This is the result of great bunches of longsuffering fruit being harvested in their lives. The blood of the martyrs is continually being poured out in countries that are resistant to the gospel. In fact, more Christians have died for their faith in this century than in all the previous centuries combined. As saints in a more peaceful land, we need to take note, lift up our brothers and sisters in prayer, and support them in other ways whenever we can.

Before I was filled with the Holy Spirit, longsuffering was a concept that never entered into my mind. I liked the quick and easy route to satisfying my desires. I bought a lot of lottery tickets, hoping to get rich. I used the "buy now and pay later" scheme many times, and I did not like to wait when making decisions about purchases. Because of blatant irresponsibility and lack of wisdom, I had to claim personal bankruptcy at the age of twenty.

I had just gotten started in life, and yet I had already managed to blow it so big. It was a hard lesson, but out of necessity I did learn to wait. In my finances today I always pray over major purchases (many times small ones, too), and then I wait on the Lord for confirmation before I spend. Frequently I feel that I am to just sit tight and not buy yet, and when I do wait patiently, I am never disappointed. Often the very item I have prayed about is delivered to my door free of charge. The Lord has taught me to pray, to stand, and then to wait on Him until He comes through for me. He hears me and is fully able to meet my need.

Behold the Lord's hand is not shortened, That it cannot save; Nor is His ear heavy, That it cannot hear.
- Isaiah 59:1

If you are in need financially, then I encourage you to learn from the Word of God what part He would have you play as a steward of God's money. Then pray the Word over your finances and stand and wait. All will be well when you put your faith in Him.

I remember an incident when I was in dire need. I operated a thrift store in a small community a few years ago, and one busy afternoon I sold a bike from the backroom for twenty dollars. Unfortunately, I did not know that my husband had taken it back there to fix it for a little boy who had paid him for the service. I was aghast. It was a newer BMX model and would cost at least a couple of hundred dollars to replace. We did not know what to do.

After work that night, we sat in our car across the street discussing the situation. Right in front of us in the window of the hardware store was a shiny, bright blue bike of a similar model and size staring out at us. My husband felt that it would be the right thing to purchase it immediately and make peace with the family. I almost gave in to the plan. It would hurt us somewhat, financially, but it seemed to be a fast and reasonable solution to the problem.

Then I had a check in my spirit —a little gentle Holy Ghost nudge that quietly told me to stand on the Word of God. I told my husband that I felt the Lord wanted us to pray and ask Him for a new bike. It had been an honest mistake to sell that little boy's prize, but we should not let the enemy have his way in the matter by stealing even more from us as a result. I said we should pray right then and have faith that God would bring us a newer and better bicycle to replace that which had been lost.

My husband thought I had lost it. At first he felt I was being totally selfish, not wanting to put out the money. He pointed out that it had been a very special and almost new model, and that we had never received such a donation before. After much debate, though, he consented to agree with me in prayer. We joined hands together and took a stand to wait upon the Lord.

The next morning I personally faced the situation with the parents who arrived to retrieve the bicycle. I humbly apologized for the mistake and promised that I would make good on the deal. I told them that I would buy the child a new bike in one week if a suitable one had not been donated in the meantime. As well, I asked them to please be patient and give us that much time, because I had asked God to bring us a new one and I wanted to give Him time to get it to us.

I will never forget the incredulous look on the mother's face. "God, is going to bring you a new bike?" she asked.

"Yes." I replied confidently.

The couple exchanged a skeptical glance and backed away reluctantly, agreeing to wait for the prescribed time.

The following morning was a Saturday, and I busily readied the store for customers. Not long after opening, a lady came in with some donations. After carrying in several boxes and bags of clothes, shoes and household items, she returned with one last thing - a beautiful royal blue BMX boy's bike, just like we had asked for. With hardly a word she turned and walked away.

Later that day the family dropped by to let me know about a bicycle sale. They were utterly amazed when I showed them the glittering new bike that the Lord had provided. It was a more exceptional model than the one that had been lost, and their son was totally excited as they left the store with it. One more happy customer for Jesus. Praise the Lord!

With many tears and much rejoicing, we told that story over and over for the next two weeks. God was glorified because we heard Him and chose to wait on Him to deliver. Yes, we could have gone out and bought a new bike; but then we would not have had a miracle. We would not have been able to exalt Jesus for His hand in it. But because we had forbearance and did not jump ahead of Him, His Name was greatly magnified all over that community as the story was retold again and again.

In my prayer life God has greatly blessed me in the area of longsuffering. He has taught me much about having patience in the last few years as I have prayed over the lost, my community and also my family.

Only four years ago, I was one of the only two professing Christians in my family. I began to stand on the Word concerning different family members occasionally as I prayed. My mom loved to socialize with people but she did not want to have anything to do with God. I prayed very specifically that friends of hers would invite her to church. Now we laugh about how many people invited her to church over those next few months. Before long, she found herself attending one of those churches. She is now saved and growing in the Lord. Praise His Holy Name!

Other family members also have received Jesus, and I continue to pray for their growth and maturity in the Word. I also stand faithfully in the gap for salvation and various blessings for uncles, aunts, grandparents and other immediate family. I do not allow the enemy to bother me with his evil reports of how one is in sin or another is involved in something. The stories he slings out at us are to make us give up hope, and I will give no ear to them. They only burden me to pray more and believe more. So, I continue to stand on the Word with longsuffering, knowing that God will answer every prayer that I ask in Jesus' Name.

"If you ask anything in My name, I will do it."
- John 14:14

As far as I am concerned, it is a done deal. They are healed, saved and set free, because I have asked my Lord to do this, and because He perfects that which concerns me.

When I first moved to my community two years ago, I was moved to pray with longsuffering for many local situations. The Lord instructed me to create a prayer list that was different for each day of the week and to be extremely disciplined in daily intercession. This was incredibly hard for me to do.

I was home-schooling my son and raising my other children while I did my own college courses at night. I was active in my church and was getting to know people in the area. It would have been so easy to let that prayer list slip, but I could not. God had told me to do it and He had filled me to overflowing with the Holy Spirit so I had the fruit of longsuffering. Even when I was exhausted or overwhelmed with a dozen other things to do, that prayer list continued to be a focused priority. God had told me to pray, and that meant whether I felt like it or not.

In the first few months there seemed to be no changes in the lives of people or organizations that were on that list. It looked to the natural eye as though nothing was happening. But God had not told me to pray only when I saw results, so I continued with longsuffering.

After a few months I began to get some positive feedback. It was always through the strangest conversations. Once, a community worker blurted out information about a person who was on my list. The gal then got embarrassed about what she had shared and apologized profusely for gossiping. I comforted her and went away praising God. She did not know it, but she had brought me important confirmation and more fuel to pray about.

I prayed intensely for intercessors to gather together, and have been greatly blessed to see three new prayer groups spring up in this area. I have also met other people who have been deeply burdened for our community for many years. God has even brought many of us together on occasion to intercede over our valley, and that has been a wonderful answer to prayer.

It is always amazing to me that when we seem to be having multiple problems, God is working out multiple solutions as we pray in faith. Last year, as I was busily doing my studies, I had a challenge that I needed to address. To complete a Bachelor of Ministry degree with my college the school requires that I have a mentor that I am accountable to. A full year had passed since I had started my courses and I could not find a mentor. I had been in my community only a short time, and most of the local pastors and lay people felt that either they did not know me well enough to make such a commitment, or that they did not have the time. I approached eight different people that met the school's criteria without having any success.

At the same time I was bathing our housing situation in prayer. When we had first moved into the valley we had rented a darling little two-bedroom house. We had been in that home about six months when our landlady decided that she wanted to sell it. She gave us the required three months notice, but during that time I was unable to find a suitable home to rent, and we did not have a sufficient down payment to buy. The rent in our town is also very high.

We looked and looked, but being a single mother with three small children was not helping. For every house that I looked at, there were at least a dozen other families looking at it as well. Landlords were cautious about renting to a single mother when they could easily find a family with two working adults.

After three months of careful searching and a lot of focused prayer, I had to take my children and stay in another community two and a half hours' drive away. Many people would have given up at that point. In fact, several of my friends and family members tried to discourage me from returning. They felt that since it was so difficult to find a home in that area we would be gladly received elsewhere. They believed that many churches would welcome the talent and education that I had, but I could not let it go. I would not let it go.

I knew that our ministry was back in that valley. I knew that my little family was called there by the Lord to do a work for Him. It had been prophesized over us, spoken over us and confirmed many times. I knew that God Himself had confirmed it to me during those many nights of prayer that I had spent on my kitchen floor while I was still living there. So I did something that seemed extremely foolish to those around me. I believed God. I did not just believe in God. I believed Him. I knew that somehow, some way, He would make it happen.

I did not get depressed and lie around doing nothing. I began to witness to those around me about Jesus. I figured that if the devil was going to try and trip me up I would make him sorry he had bothered. Over the next eight weeks the Lord used me to bring eight people to Jesus. Glory to God! I also found an excellent church with a Holy Ghost-filled pastor and an on-fire congregation. As I worked to tie the new believers into that church, God began to build a strong friendship between that pastor and myself.

During that time I continued to complete my studies and mother my children. I also drove back to the valley every week or two to look for a home. Finally, the Lord opened an unexpected doorway.

My mother's husband-to-be had been watching our persistent efforts. The Holy Spirit in me had impressed him as he daily witnessed our joy, our love for others, and the peace of our family even in the midst of upheaval. He respected the stand that I had taken to return to our community and he decided to help us purchase a home.

In the fall we returned to the valley. We now live in an almost new mobile home with a big yard right in the center of where we wanted to be. God has met every financial need that we have had and more. Even better than all of that, the Lord also supplied me with a mentor and friend as a result of our layover in that other community.

As we settled into our home a year ago I began to pray again for this valley. One of the key prayers was that I would meet my neighbors. I had just moved into the trailer court, knew only three families in the town, and had briefly met a couple that lived in the court. After praying for only a couple of weeks I excitedly realized one evening that we had already met and established relationships with sixteen families right around our home. Over the winter we got to know many of them better, and from those we have recently been privileged to lead five people to the Lord.

Our work here is now well established and growing. We started a home church early in the spring and have now grown too large for our mobile home. We now meet in a local hall every Sunday afternoon to worship the Lord. People are growing and maturing in the things of God. They are being transformed by the power of the Holy Ghost. All praise and honor and glory be unto the Lamb!

Longsuffering is a fruit of the Holy Spirit. When we are filled to overflowing we have a knack for patience to wait upon the Lord. As we have an appetite for the things of God, we learn to hear His voice. When we know that we know, that we know, that He has told us to stand firm, we show incredible fortitude for answers to prayer. That kind of patience works well with faith and that kind of faith our Lord loves to respond to.

May the Holy Ghost continue to fill you and overflow through you as you read. May you be blessed by His presence, and may the fruit of longsuffering become manifest in your life. May the Lord strengthen you to wait upon Him for the answers to your prayers. In Jesus' Name I pray this blessing over you.

Amen.

EIGHT

Gentleness

There has been a total transformation in every area of my life since the Holy Ghost took over, but when some people meet me they may still feel that I could use some work on the fruit of gentleness. Everyone who is filled to overflowing with the Holy Spirit is going to manifest good fruit in each of the nine character attributes that are listed in Galatians. However, how that plays out in each individual's life will vary based on their own personality and the individual giftings that they have been given by God.

One of my personal giftings is boldness. When I was not saved, I used that gifting to lead others into sin with me. When I was changed by the power of God, that boldness became a powerful tool for evangelism. In order to adequately judge my transformation in the area of gentleness we need to look carefully at the before and the after picture.

Gentleness used to be an unknown concept to me. In that one word I can sum up a whole truck load of change that took place in my life.

Before the Holy Spirit transformed me I would not have been your first choice to invite to a dinner party. I would have arrived late enough to make a spectacular entrance at your black jacket affair. I would have been wearing a glittering red dress, spiked heels (and hair) and red lipstick, with a different sort of gaudy affair attached to my right arm. I would have smoked while I spilled my party drinks, talked way too loudly about inappropriate topics, and embarrassed even the hired help with my lewdness. There was not one gentle bone in me.

I did not know, nor did I care that a gentle answer would turn away wrath. In fact, I liked a good fight. I would have been the one in the bathroom at the end of the evening pulling another guest's hair and swearing like a trucker.

Looking back on it all now I realize how ridiculous I looked, but at the time I had no clue. I thought that being gentle was a weakness, and I did not want to look weak in front of anyone.

That was pure pride. I wanted to look tough. Never show weakness.

Now I understand that gentleness does not show weakness. Rather, it shows great strength. Anyone can flip out and scream obscenities, but it takes real character to stand in the face of opposition with a smile and turn the other cheek.

When the devil comes to rattle our cage he is looking for us to fight with him. He wants us to enter into the wrestling ring of sin with him. Satan wants our indignation to rise up in us. He taunts us to respond, "You can't do that. I have rights!" or "How dare you. Who do you think you are? I will sue!"

Satan just laughs at us when we play his games even with his own equipment on. He tempts us to use our fists, physical weapons and law suits to get our own way. There is no gentleness in any of those things. There is no humility. There is no room for God to intervene. We have taken on God's job of vengeance and have therefore made ourselves out to be God.

Although I knew it was not the Lord's way to fight and argue and threaten, I seemed powerless to stop myself. Even after the outburst of wrath was over, I still had great difficulty going and facing the mess that I had made. I made excuses for myself and justified my actions. I thought, "He deserved it. He started it," or, "I sure showed her."

I might have thought it felt good to blow up at the time, but it sure did not feel good later. I had no peace at night and no friends the next day.

When the Lord got a hold of me and the Holy Ghost filled me to overflowing, gentleness came much more naturally. I did not notice it immediately because it was a gentle change. It was subtle, but it did underline every aspect of my life. Looking back now I can see that it began in those early weeks of walking with Jesus, anointed by His Spirit.

One of the most evident changes was the way that I felt about my children. Before the transformation, I had bought the world's lies about my children. I loved them, but they kind of got in my way. There were all kinds of things that I wanted to do and couldn't because I had kids. I was often short with my eldest in his first two years, but after God came into my life and took over, I could not get enough of my kids. I more than just loved them. I wanted to sow into them. I frequently even today plan ways to teach them about God and look for ways to impact them for His kingdom. I see my role with my children more clearly. They are my number one mission field. On my own I may lead a few hundred people to Jesus in my lifetime, but my kids could impact nations. I remind myself that Billy Graham had a mother too. So, I view them a lot differently than I used to.

I also mother them in different ways. They get lots of love. There is an abundance of hugs, kisses and tickling. There is also some firmness and discipline, but it is never in anger. It has to be done, so it is taken care of. Then there is gentleness as we later discuss the matter.

There is gentleness as I home-school them. I love to watch them as they learn their colors and discover how to read and write. It is such a thrill to see their minds grasping mathematical concepts. As I read them stories I watch their faces and enjoy their expressions. I try to regularly take a special time with each of them individually one on one as well. Sometimes I let one of them stay up later than the other two and we will watch our favorite evangelist for a while, all snuggled up on the sofa. I let them pick, and you would be amazed at their choices. They are all names that you would recognize.

It is fun to be a mother, and it is gentle too. It is the gentlest thing that I have ever done. I like this Scripture because to me it defines gentleness better than anything that I can say.

But we were gentle among you, just as a nursing mother cherishes her own children.
- 1 Thessalonians 2:7

That says it all. Remember when that baby was so small and so fragile that we just knew that we had to be gentle with him or her? Just thinking about it now we can remember the way the baby's hair smelled and the softness of his or her skin. That is how it is supposed to be with our children, even as they grow. They are precious. We should not destroy them with our wrath. We should love them with gentleness, and we should be that way with others as well.

The apostle Paul explained this in his letter to the church at Thessalonica. He was gentle with the whole congregation of men, women and children.

That is what a Christian is supposed to be. Gentle.
That is how a leader is supposed to teach. Gently.

> *And a servant of the Lord must not
> quarrel but be gentle to all, able to
> teach, patient, in humility correcting
> those who are in opposition...*
> - 2 Timothy 2:24,25a

This does not mean that we avoid controversial
topics when they need to be addressed. Paul did not
avoid discussing sexual sin nor did he shy away
from teaching on finances or proper conduct. His
teaching was gentle, yet firm, and it was apt for the
occasion.

We need to teach from the uncompromising word
of God even if it is not popular. But when we do it
with gentleness and humility it is received. People
come under conviction and see something in us that
they want to have. They are tired of screaming at
their kids and their spouses. They want to have
gentleness.

Gentleness is a fruit of the Holy Spirit. We do
not receive it by praying for it. We get the fruit by
receiving the Holy Spirit. It is more of the outpouring. When we are full of the Spirit, it is natural to
bear the Spirit's fruit in abundance.

We will not win the battles of this life by taking
up the devil's weapons. God has given us special
tools to defeat the wiles of our enemy, and they are

the instruments of gentleness and peace. They are truth, righteousness, the gospel of peace, faith, salvation, the Word of God and prayer.

Stand therefore, having girded your waist with truth, having put on the breastplate of righteousness, and having shod your feet with the preparation of the gospel of peace; above all, taking the shield of faith with which you will be able to quench all the fiery darts of the wicked one. And take the helmet of salvation, and the sword of the Spirit, which is the word of God; praying always with all prayer and supplication in the Spirit, being watchful to this end with all perseverance and supplication for all the saints...
- Ephesians 6:14-18

These are the weapons that take the nations for Jesus. These gentle, but strong, weapons rock our communities into change. They impact our families and bring in the lost, and they break the yoke of bondage. These are the gentle armaments that every Christian needs to learn to wield with skill.

Paul likens each of these character attributes to a part of a Roman soldier's attire. They are each a powerful asset to the Christian's life, but compared to the alternative, they are weapons of gentleness—gentle tools that, when placed in the hands of a Spirit-filled believer, become powerful implements of God's army.

When that driver accosts us with angry hand signals we need to respond with gentleness, giving him or her a huge smile in our rear view mirror. At the school board meeting we need to be bearers of truth, making our stand for righteousness in a gentle and humble manner. When someone withholds money from us that we have rightfully earned, we do not need to rant and rave and threaten. Rather, we need to go behind closed doors and speak the Word of God over the situation and stand in faith that the Lord will look after it. Most of all, we need to be people of prayer, not people of wrath and revenge.

Gentleness may be a less noticeable fruit on the Spirit-filled tree, but it is extremely delectable to the taste buds. It is a fruit that you may never have considered before because it is quiet and inconspicuous next to the more obvious cherries of choice. It does not glitter like joy, or summon like love, but it is there hanging with all of the others for a very good reason. Like a banana, it blends all of the other flavors very well together in a delicious fruit smoothie. Without it we would be very bland indeed.

If you are reading this and lack gentleness in your life, spend more time soaking in the presence of the Most High God. Gentleness is fruit that grows on a Spirit-filled tree.

I pray for you right now that you will continue to be filled with the Holy Spirit and bear much gentleness in your life. I ask the Mighty Counselor to teach you how to use your gentle weaponry with effectiveness and power. May gentleness blend together with all of the other fruit of the Spirit in your life and flow out of you over everyone that you meet. May it influence your family and impact strangers, and may it never run dry in you again.

In Jesus' Name, I pray.

Amen.

NINE

Goodness

*W*hen a person receives the Holy Spirit they may begin to manifest the fruit of goodness in their lives very quickly.

When I was a mediocre, lukewarm Christian I understood goodness. I wanted to help all kinds of people and do the good thing, yet I was powerless to follow through with longsuffering, and my love did not last for the unlovable. I frequently chose to do the good thing but I was not able to maintain that stand under trial or temptation.

Once I was filled to overflowing, goodness oozed out of me. I wanted to save the world. I ran thrift shops to help single mothers. I baked cookies for the church bazaar, and I sat on the board of a Christian organization. I got very busy doing good things. Then I began to realize that it is not my job to save the world. That job belongs to Jesus. It is my job to listen to Him, and to do what He tells me to do. It is not my job to burn myself out on every good thing that comes along and then have nothing left to serve my Lord.

A gifting called discernment began to kick in, and I discovered with the help of my Mighty Counselor that there are "good things" and then there are "God things." If I would hearken my ear to do the things that He called me to do, then I would not wear myself out on all of my good ideas.

> *And it shall come to pass, if thou shalt hearken diligently unto the voice of the Lord thy God, to observe and to do all his commandments which I command thee this day, that the Lord thy God will set thee on high above all nations of the earth: And all these blessings shall come on thee, and overtake thee, if thou shalt hearken unto the voice of the Lord thy God.*
> *- Deuteronomy 28:1-2 (KJV)*

I have been blessed with an abundance of good ideas. Unfortunately, if I try to run several businesses, a couple of ministries, my household, and chew bubblegum all at the same time, my teeth will fall out! I am just not built that way, and neither are you. We need to stop being "superperson" for a minute and learn to listen to God.

I used to think that if I could not do six things at once then I must be a failure. It never occurred to me that God could bless me if I did fewer good things and more God things, but that is what happened.

The Holy Spirit began to teach me that when too many things were happening, and it was all spinning out of control, I needed to give up control. I needed to go spend some time reading the Word of God. He taught me to read it, to do it, and to apply it to everything. That was one way I could hearken diligently to His voice. He taught me to spend that time reading and then to look for ways to be a doer of the Word in my day-to-day activities.

But be doers of the word, and not hearers only, deceiving yourselves.
- James 1:22

My Teacher showed me that it was not as important to run an organization as it was to raise my children in the Lord. He showed me that I needed to spend more time in His presence than in front of the television. He directed me to feed my spirit with Christian books, videos and sermon tapes regularly, so that I would always be filled, filled, filled with the Holy Ghost. In this way I have been ready to minister to the lost whenever the opportunity presents itself. Out of a full cup I have been able to pour peace, joy and hope into the lives of others in the middle of crisis, making a difference for the kingdom of God. Praise the Lord!

For two years Jesus took me off of every board I had been part of so that He could teach me how to pray. He taught me how to stand in faith and wait upon Him with longsuffering. He flowed a river of love into me until it ran over and over. He taught me to listen to His voice and to distinguish it from all others.

He taught me these things not because I was special, or smart, or attractive. By the world's standards I was a very poor choice indeed. I was a single mother from a sordid background. My society looked upon me as the weakest member and yet God decided to use me mightily.

> *For you see your calling, brethren, that not many wise according to the flesh, not many mighty, not many noble, are called. But God has chosen the foolish things of the world to put to shame the wise, and God has chosen the weak things of the world to put to shame the things which are mighty...*
>
> *- 1 Corinthians 1:26*

There is only one reason why God uses me for anything. It is because of that commitment that I made when I gave my life totally over to Him. It was in that prayer that I confessed in Chapter One. I have not been good at many things in my life, but when I gave it all to Jesus I held nothing back. I gave Him everything and I have continued to be obedient to seek Him first above all things even until now.

> *"Has the Lord as great delight in burnt offerings and sacrifices, As in obeying the voice of the Lord? Behold, to obey is better than sacrifice, And to heed than the fat of rams."*
> *- 1 Samuel 15:22*

Obedience is everything.

God loves our obedience more than our sacrifices. I have chosen to obey Him in a day-to-day stewardship. I do not try to impress Him with large financial sacrifices once a year and then pray for a blessing to meet some miracle need. I tithe off of the gross of every cent that comes my way, then I give above that as He directs me. Even the sacrifices that I make are out of obedience when He guides me. As a result, we have a consistent flow of financial miracles that meet every need, and God is continually glorified as I praise Him and testify publicly of all that He does for us. (By the way, I have praised Him publicly even when we were wondering where the miracles were.)

The Holy Spirit has prompted me to be obedient even when nobody is looking. He has made me confess sin to my Lord and also to others when necessary. He has motivated me to be obedient to read the Word when I have not felt like it, and encouraged me to pray when I was too tired. Even in the middle of busyness, obedience is a good thing, and it is a God thing too.

When we are obedient, we realize that our prayer life and the time we spend in the presence of the Most High God is a priority over everything else. So many times people ask me "How do you know the voice of the Lord?"

How do the sheep know the shepherd's voice? They spend time in that quiet pasture listening to Him.

When we read the Word over and over again God is writing it on the tablet of our hearts. When we meditate on the Scriptures, we contemplate His ways and we do not forget His Word. From reading the Bible and praying, and from just sitting in His presence, we begin to know His voice. The more time we spend in His pasture the clearer we understand Him.

After we have spent a lot of time with our shepherd He will begin to speak to us in our daily situations. We know His voice if we have soaked in His presence. If we have not spent that time reading His Word and praying we will be easily deceived.

Satan sometimes comes in and stealthily twists the Word. It almost sounds right, but not quite. If we have read the Word a lot, we can tell immediately if it is a little off, and we know to rebuke him in the Name of Jesus. The cults prey on Christians who are weak in the Word of God. Their number one area of growth comes from Christians who have been born into their faith but not raised up in it. They exploit subjects like the Trinity because they know that most believers know this as a matter of faith, but have not researched it for themselves. These saints are easily led astray because they have not learned to carefully listen to the voice of their Shepherd by spending time in His Word.

Another trick of the enemy is to get us to make a rushed decision. "Buy it now!" "React right now!" "Hurry, hurry!" "Do it quick!"

The Lord's voice is very different. He says, "Wait upon Me," and "Be still, and know that I Am God."

Sometimes I get one of my great ideas to do something good. It may be a youth outreach, an extra church service, or even to invite somebody over to dinner. God has taught me, though, that my time is precious. All of those things are good things, but if they are not God's idea for right now, then I need to lay them aside until He releases me to do them. He sees everything, and may know a better way to do that good thing or a better time to go ahead with it. He may even know someone else who is better equipped for that job or even called to perform it. I have learned that, when I get a good idea, the first thing I need to do is to soak it in prayer. I then lift it up to the Lord several times over a week or longer. I listen for that gentle prompting in my spirit, and then if I feel He is telling me "Yes," I ask Him for confirmation.

If it is about an upcoming event I may ask the Lord to pull together all of the people and cover the needs quickly so that I will know that it is His will. I tell Him that, if it is not His will for right now, He needs to close every door in my face, so that I will not get caught up in good ideas that are not God's ideas.

If it is concerning a decision that I need to make, I ask Jesus to bring me confirmation through one of my Spirit-filled friends or my mentor. Often when it is a God idea I do not even need to bring it up to them. The Holy Spirit is the same for me and for everyone else as well. A friend may call me the following morning and tell me that she was praying for me in the night and she needed to give me a Scripture that she received from the Lord. She may then read to me the exact quotation that I had been standing on concerning that situation. This kind of thing has happened countless times as I have learned to lean on Him and trust not in my own understanding.

When we are submitted to God He will speak to us clearly. There is no reason to read between the lines or to look for signs in the sky. We do not need some organization to interpret the will of God for our lives. We need to read the Word daily, meditate on it, and pray fervently.

Spending time with Jesus is the top priority. We cannot minister to others effectively out of an empty cup. If we try, we are working out of our flesh. We spin our wheels in the mud and get more and more frustrated wondering why it is not working. "Why don't people listen to me? Why are they not being transformed? Why are things falling apart? Why? Why? Why?"

If we want to bear a lot of good fruit and do a lot of good things that really matter, then we need to be plugged into our source. The fruit of the Spirit grows on a tree that is firmly planted in good soil, drinking the living water of Jesus Christ. We are to be regularly plugged into Him for our weather forecast, not CBN. In this way we will always have more than enough, rain or shine.

When we are blessed with His goodness, then we will bear the fruit of goodness and bless others. We will prosper so that we can in turn prosper others. We will be like a well-watered tree next to a river that bears fruit in its season.

Blessed is the man who walks not in the counsel of the ungodly, Nor stands in the path of sinners, Nor sits in the seat of the scornful; But his delight is in the law of the Lord, And in His law he meditates day and night. He shall be like a tree Planted by the rivers of water, That brings forth its fruit in its season, Whose leaf also shall not wither; And whatever he does shall prosper.
- Psalm 1:1-3

We need to be so plugged in to Jesus that doing the good thing is natural to us, but doing the God thing is everything to us.

May the Holy Spirit give you much discernment as you carefully determine that which He has called you to do. May He release you to do those things that He requires of you, and may He release you from those things that He does not. I pray that the fruit of goodness will grow abundantly on your tree as you are well-watered by your source in Jesus. May the Holy Spirit continue to overflow in and around you as you go deeper into your relationship with Him.

In Jesus' Name I pray.

Amen.

TEN

Faith And Faithfulness

Many unbelievers have difficulty with stories in the Bible. They question the miracles of creation, Jonah and the fish, and Moses parting the Red sea. This is one area that I never personally had a problem with. Even before my conversion, I believed all those miracles and all of the other Bible stories as well. As a child, I had read them from my Grandmother's big collection of Bible storybooks, and I just knew that they were true. As I later grew and began to read the Word I still did not question that God had done those things, but I did question whether or not God would do those things for me. I believed in God, but I had not yet begun to believe Him when it came to my own needs.

Faith and faithfulness are God's ideas. They are attributes of His character and natural for Him to

pour out on us. Jesus is the author and the finish-
er of our faith, and He causes us to grow in that
faith as we submit to His leading.

Over the years I have learned two very important
things about faith that I believe that every believer
can benefit from.

First of all, God clearly tells us how to get more
faith if we are lacking in that department.

 *So then faith comes by hearing, and
hearing by the word of God.*
- Romans 10:17

We get more faith by hearing the Word, not just
by reading the Word. Reading the Word is important because if we have read the Word then we will
know the voice of our Savior when He speaks to us.
However, faith does not come by reading the
Word—it comes by hearing the Word.

In Greek, "Rhema" is used in the place of "Word".
This is also very significant. Rhema is the spoken
Word of God. It is heard audibly by the listener and
is spoken either by God Himself or through His servant. The same Rhema is used in Acts as Paul
spoke a word and then continued to quote the
prophet Isaiah as a divine word of knowledge over
the situation.

So when they did not agree among themselves, they departed after Paul had said one word: "The Holy Spirit spoke rightly through Isaiah the prophet to our fathers..."
- Acts 28:25

The Rhema Word can also be the preached Word.

"The word is near you, in your mouth and in your heart," (that is, the word of faith which we preach)...
- Romans 10:8b

Peter used the word Rhema to describe the preaching of the Gospel.

Now this is the word by which the gospel was preached to you.
1 Peter 1:25b

The Rhema Word of God is the spoken Word of God. That is why sinners come under conviction and the lost are saved when an evangelist shares the Gospel. That is why a congregation is impacted to grow while listening to the pastor preach the Sunday sermon. These events should be commonly taking place in Christian meetings across our land.

Unfortunately, many times we are instead hearing quaint stories from the pulpit that are no more the Rhema Word of God than the morning newspaper. Why is that? It is because it is lacking the second aspect of faith that needs to be implemented in the lives of believers. All believers, even pastors, need this aspect of faith if they are going to utter the Rhema Word of God. We need to be filled to overflowing with the Holy Spirit. Faithfulness is a fruit of the Spirit. It is poured out into the heart and the mouth of the believer in great abundance when we are experiencing outpour.

Birthing faith is like birthing a watermelon. It is huge—you would notice it! If a watermelon were growing on a tree, it would make the branches bend under its weight. It would take up so much space that it would be clearly evident to all who passed by. People would stop and stare at the extraordinary sight of a great, juicy, delicious watermelon hanging amongst the pears, cherries and bananas of our Spirit-filled tree. Faith is noticeable.

When a believer gets sick and chooses to have faith to live instead of to die, people notice. Some people do not understand, but they notice. When a Christian stands on the Word of God for finances and begins to prosper, then people notice. They may react out of suspicion or jealousy, but they sure do notice.

A monstrous watermelon is as hard to miss as a new Cadillac on the front drive. Faith is a powerful fruit that changes circumstances and then begins to grow a harvest of results.

When I first got filled to overflowing I was in the middle of a very ugly financial crisis. That was what had driven me to my knees in the first place. NEED. I was totally broken and had nowhere to look but up.

When I gave myself over to Jesus the Holy Spirit-filled me up, and faith grew instantly on my tree. He taught me to tithe and give faithfully out of the very little that I had, and then He grew a crop right before my eyes. Jesus was not impressed by my need, but my faith changed everything.

I remember one day in those early weeks when my three-year-old came and tugged on my leg, asking me for a snack. I went to the refrigerator and opened it up, staring gloomily into the bare interior. I stood there with that sinking feeling of desperation in my gut, not knowing what to tell my little boy who was looking up at me so expectantly.

Then faith rose up in me like a flood and I began to feel the Rhema Word of God swell within my spirit. I spoke to that fridge in the Name of Jesus and told it to be filled. Then I looked up to God and said, "Lord, I am Your servant, and I have been learning to be faithful as You have been teaching me from Your Word. I have been obedient; therefore this is not my problem. I will not worry about it. This is Your situation and I give it to You. I need $50 for groceries today and I am asking You for it, knowing that all I ask in Jesus' Name I shall receive!"

Then I slammed the refrigerator door shut and walked away from it.

Half an hour later there was a knock on my door. A friend was walking by and remembered he needed to make an important phone call. He was supposed to call an evangelist that we both knew to make plans for the upcoming weekend. During the conversation with him, the evangelist asked my friend if he knew how to get a hold of me. The evangelist then told my friend that just before the phone had rang he had been praying and the Lord had just told him that I needed $50, and he was wondering how to get it to me!

Praise the Lord! God is faithful!

I had that money in my hands within a couple of hours and we had everything that we needed. In those early months of walking with Jesus He met every need that we had. In those days we needed over $2000 a month just to live, and we started many months knowing where only a few hundred dollars was coming from. However, the Lord knew just where to pull that fish out of the water. People we did not even know often brought us food and clothes, and even gave us money. More importantly, God showed me how to work to serve Him, and He caused me to prosper in the work of my hands. We can believe in Him, and then we can believe Him for our needs as well.

I have been young, and now am old; yet I have not seen the righteous forsaken, nor his descendents begging bread.
- Psalm 37:25

Blessed is the Lord Most High. As I learned to seek Him first He added all those other things unto me as well.

The Lord began to move in my life in the area of faith in many different ways. The Word of God would come alive to me as I read it. Many times the gentle prompting of the Holy Spirit would wake me in the middle of the night. "Get up, and read My Word," He would tell me. Sometimes He would say, "I have something that I want to show you."

I would sit for hours in His presence reading His Word and listening to Him confirm it to my heart.

Faith was growing in me. Bushels and bushels of watermelon-sized faith. He showed me that His Word is everlasting and does not change. He taught me that what He has done for one person He will do for another who obeys Him in the same way. I read the story of Elijah calling down fire from heaven and it took on a new meaning in the light of Rhema revelation. I read the story of Deborah and Barak and knew that God could use a woman like me too. I read the story of Balaam's donkey and knew that I, too, could be used to speak the Rhema Word of God.

Faith rose up in me like a mighty gushing fountain that could not be shut off. If the devil tried to stop up the fountain with his finger, the pipes just rattled and sprang holes. Faith gushed everywhere over my life. I began to declare the Word of God with boldness over every situation. I began to regularly lead people to Jesus everywhere that I went. God began to use me to speak words of knowledge even over strangers. They would weep when I would share a message from the Lord about a subject that I had absolutely no way of knowing, without God Himself telling me. People changed as a result. I began to pray with power and miracles began to happen.

Once, during a Bible study at my home, a twelve-year-old boy fell off his roller blades in my backyard. Two adults carried him into the room and he lay moaning and crying. His leg was twisted and jutted out in a crazy contortion just below the knee. It was swelling so rapidly that his wide leg trousers were tight around his lower calf. Faith rose up in me like a mountain. I commanded everyone to praise God and I spoke in tongues for a couple of minutes raising my hands in the air to my Master in heaven. I spoke Rhema Words of faith, declaring Scriptures of healing, and then laid my hands upon that boy's leg in the Name of Jesus. The swelling instantly disappeared beneath my hands as they visibly sunk inches toward the wound. The women in the room began to weep at the sight of it. I held my hands there for a few minutes, taking authority over the pain and asking God, who created those bones, to knit them back together in wholeness.

When I lifted my hands we saw that Jesus had

done a miracle! The leg was totally healed. The boy had stopped crying and sat in wonder, moving his leg about with ease and hugging his mother in joy. We then helped him to his feet, completely healed by the power of the Holy Spirit and the Name of Jesus. Hallelujah! Glory to God! He is awesome!

After a believer is used of God in such a miraculous way, everything changes. Faith changes everything. Nothing is impossible for those who know God.

Faith is a tool that our Lord gives to those who know Him so they will use it to bring glory to His Name. Faith was used in Biblical times and it still works today.

Some say that a faith ministry is not for them. Their ministry is inner-city soup kitchens. However, the lost who come to them need a touch of faith. They need a miracle. We need the Holy Ghost outpouring in our own lives so that we can be used of God to give them that miracle. Faith without a manifestation of God's power is of little use to someone on drugs. They need to know that it works so they can have hope.

But someone will say, "You have faith, and I have works." Show me your faith without your works, and I will show you my faith by my works. You believe that there is one God. You do well.

Even the demons believe — and trem-ble! But do you want to know O fool-ish man, that faith without works is dead?

- James 2:18-20

Miracles come by prayers of faith. Answers come by prayers of faith.

God is not moved by need. If He were, there would be no starving people on this planet. God is moved by faith. I have tried living my life in doubt and I have tried living it with faith. Faith is much better. I highly recommend it.

I thank God that He fills me up to overflowing just about every day. I thank Him for the extraordinary fruit of faith that He has produced on my Spirit-filled tree. It is one of the fruit that I treasure the most. It is all about Him. It is totally centered on Him. It is for His glory and because of His faithfulness. It is so profound and yet so simple. With childlike faith I just believe God and it is well with my soul.

Heavenly Father, I pray right now over the reader of this book that You will give them a hunger and a zeal for the written Word of God. May they never be satisfied with only a little bit. Lord, I ask You to make it come alive in their heart and in their mouth. May You speak the Rhema Word into their ears and have it penetrate the very depths of their being. May You bring Spirit-filled men and women into their life to preach and teach the Rhema Word regularly, as well. Jesus, I ask also that You fill them more and more with the Holy Spirit. Give this person an abundant overflow of giant watermelon-sized faith that will grow on their tree and be a spectacle to the world around them. May their faith move mountains, and heal nations and individuals, all to Your glory. In Your precious Name, Jesus, I pray and ask these things.

Amen.

ELEVEN

Random Acts Of Christian Kindness

There are many people who want to do good and kind things in this world. That is why we have law enforcement officers, firefighters, health care professionals, clergy and other helping occupations. Often they start out full of zeal in their profession—eager to make a difference, but unfortunately that passion usually fades as the years pass. They are faced with case after case of hopelessness, and the work wears them down. Many people even forget their initial motivation and their work becomes just a paycheck. As a result, those who are really in need can be met by stony expressions, or even outright hostility, by the people who should be there to help.

Occasionally I run into a community worker who is Spirit-filled and I can immediately tell the difference. They are joyful and eager to help. They move a little faster, listen a little harder and smile a lot more. Because they are plugged into their source they are never worn right out and empty.

That is the difference. When we are filled with the Holy Spirit we always have something to give. Our cup overfloweth.

I always wanted to help people, but before Jesus took over my life I did not really know how. I was so empty myself that I did not have anything left over to give. Usually I just became another leech to suck them dry.

After the Holy Spirit transformed me, my acts of kindness actually started to work. Very shortly I was being used by God to be a real blessing to some very needy people. It was such an exciting time as I learned the power of random acts of kindness.

During that time I had been studying the Bible about finances, giving, stewardship and wealth. The Word was coming alive to me, God was showing me daily how to improve my situation, and He was blessing me abundantly. I was rejoicing in this and sharing regularly with other Christians that I knew.

One day another single mother invited me over to her house for lunch after church. She had made a huge pot of chili that she served in plastic margarine containers because she had no bowls. We sat on a rough wooden board over two pails and I noticed that there were not proper curtains on the windows. After lunch, the children played in the living room and my son complained that the sofa had bit him. I then saw that the springs were poking up. Later, when I used the washroom, I noticed that there was not proper bedding on the beds and that towels were also badly needed. Just before we left she told me that she did not have a vacuum cleaner and that she was sweeping the carpet to keep it clean.

I went home that night grieving in my spirit. I wanted to do something for her so badly, but I did not have much to give her. I too, was a single mother, although I was not in the same state of affairs that she was in. However, I realized that if I had not submitted to the Lord I could have ended up that way, or even worse.

This blessed woman of God was not what the world would call a welfare bum. She worked two jobs, but her daycare expenses took half her money. The rest was eaten up by rent, food and utilities. Like many single mothers, she did not receive any child support from the father of her children. He had divorced her years earlier, and she had not heard from him since.

Over the years, when something broke down or got lost in moving (single moms move frequently looking for a better situation or escaping a bad one), she just learned to go without that item. She did not smoke. She did not do drugs. She did not drink alcohol, and yet she was in dire need.

This story is not as uncommon as one might think. Over the years I have met many single mothers who show up to church all dressed nice on Sunday, but later I was shocked to realize the poverty they lived in at home. They wear the one good outfit they own and come with a smile so nobody asks any questions. But we need to start asking questions. We need to get to know these people and show some kindness.

I did not have anything to give her, but I decided that I would ask God for all that she needed. She was a Christian, but she did not know about financial matters. So, I did some Bible studies with her and prayed that God would supply her needs for her. I also began to pray for other single mothers that I knew. Then I talked to a few people about an idea that I had. I mentioned to four people over the next week that I wanted to collect items in my garage to help needy families.

That week I attended a church meeting where a prophet pointed me out in the audience. He said, "The Lord wants to tell you that He is about to pour out on you such a blessing that you will not have room enough to receive it!"

That Saturday I got a phone call from somebody who had heard about my idea. This precious couple had just helped their mother go into a home for the elderly. The family was not in need of most of her furniture or personal items, and it was the lady's wish that her things would be a blessing to someone who needed them. Would I be interested?

That evening seven truckloads of furniture, clothing, household items and dishes were delivered to my garage. I did not have room enough to receive them. The following afternoon more trucks arrived from another source.

Many pieces of clothing still had price tags on them.

I went right to work sorting. There were outfits with matching shoes in my new friend's size. There was a boot box full of brand new pantyhose (something that single moms often do without). There were curtains, bedding, nightgowns, towels, dishes, chairs, a sofa, and even a vacuum cleaner. I was like a kid at Christmas time!

The next day after church I asked some people to help me, and we delivered a whole truck load to that one single mother. I will never forget the look on her face. She stood on her step with tears running down her cheeks in shock and disbelief as men carried everything into her house and then stayed to help haul away the old stuff.

It was a great day to serve the Lord! Praise His Holy Name! He is Awesome!

Over the next several months there were many families that were blessed by that ministry. It was a time of learning, growth and blessing for me, as well.

We picked up people and took them to church activities and soup kitchens. We prayed over the sick and stood in the gap for the lost. We delivered badly needed items and groceries, and the blessings continued to pour in from every direction.

I took an information sheet around to garage sales as they were closing. I would explain who I was and what I was doing. I told them that we were not a non-profit organization. We were just a few Christian people who had gathered together to help the needy. If they chose to donate to us, their goods would be given to mostly single parent families. What we did not have an immediate need for; we would sell to cover costs. When this was explained, the people gave generously. They told their neighbors about it, as well, and when we would come with a truck there were often twice as many things there. They also blessed me personally. Many times they tucked money into my hands as I left and told me that I could spend it on anything that I needed for myself or my ministry. Others came out and volunteered. It was a very exciting time!

It was usually very rewarding work, but not always. Women who have been hurt can become calloused and mean. Like an animal that has been kicked too often, they can unexpectedly turn on you. Occasionally we would furnish a whole house and then be indefinitely ignored.

People also came from different backgrounds and I had to learn to be gracious. I would take some dear lady to church who was dressed in a mini skirt and tank top, smoking, swearing, and yelling at her kids as we went. But the Lord had warned me not to try and clean these fish before we had caught them. So I just loved on them the way they were.

Other Christians asked me how I coped with discouragement. Honestly, I can say that from that time right up until now I have never had to cope with any discouragement. I have never had any. Sure, there are setbacks, but there are always three things that shield me from burn out.

First of all, I know my mission. Whatever God has called me to, I know it. I have spent much time in His presence and I know His voice, His plan, and His purpose for me. This is tremendously freeing. I am able to determine quickly if a new idea is going to fit into His plan or if it is something that will inevitably draw me away from it. I also understand that it is not my calling to change people. I am called to help people, but it is not my job to clean them up. That job belongs to the Holy Spirit. It is my calling to show people the unconditional love of Jesus and to show them by example how to be plugged into that source. He gets to do all of the miracles. Praise the Lord!

Secondly, I have a mountain of faith. When I give to somebody who does seem to receive it well, I do not get hung up on that. Even if that mom never sees us again, for the next several years her children will remember every time they sit on that couch that it was delivered courtesy of Jesus Christ. There is precious seed in planting kindness. I pray over that seed, and it will be watered, protected and given light by my Lord. Someday I will rejoice again in heaven as I see the marvelous harvest that God brought forth as a result. Kindness is a "big picture" plan that we need to look at with long range vision.

Thirdly, and most importantly, I never suffer from burn out because I am filled with Holy Ghost power and outpour. I am like the "Energizer Bunny" of joy! I just can't help myself. Sometimes I wake up in the middle of the night because I am just too excited to sleep. As I spend quiet time with my Lord He is faithful to pour into me and fill me to overflowing with juicy fruit. It is really amazing, and I highly recommend it!

The best cure for burn out, stress, depression, discouragement, mental fatigue or physical tiredness is an injection of Holy Ghost power. When we are worn out we need to go to church more, not less. We need to spend some time on our faces praising God or crying out to Him. We should turn on our favorite television evangelist and stir ourselves up. Get excited! Greater is He who lives in us than He who lives in the world! We need to look like this is true, because it is true. As we are filled up we can pour out. Kindness is natural to someone who is full of the Holy Spirit.

There are many places that we can display acts of kindness. We live in a very needy world. We are surrounded by the hurting and the lost. We can reach out to them right where we are, and we do not have to wait for a special time of the year either. It is wonderful to do random charitable acts at Christmas, but people suffer all year long. Let's be a blessing whenever the Lord leads us.

Throughout God's Word, He especially points out the cause of the widows and the fatherless. In our society adults live long, so we do not have many widows physically, but spiritually we have several. Women and children have been abandoned, discarded and used up. These women may have made a poor choice, or they may have left a relationship when they should not have. Sometimes they have had to leave for their own safety or for the safety of their children. Whatever the reason, we need to stop judging and start helping.

Single mothers are often hungry for the Gospel. They are looking for answers. Give them some love and some kindness. Give them some mentoring and read them Isaiah chapter 54. Jesus will do a miracle.

We look for ways to send missionaries to Africa or even to soup kitchens within our inner cities. These are great ministries, but we need to help those across the street first. Right here in our own backyards, we have people who need Jesus. Our Lord is just as concerned for their souls as He is for those who live in distant lands.

Some of those who need our help are already Christians. They are attending Sunday services and hungry for more. They need to be raised up in the things of God, uplifted and assisted as we are led.

Therefore, as we have opportunity, let us do good to all, especially to those who are of the household of faith.
                          - Galatians 6:10

Ladies, I encourage you, if you are a Spirit-filled believer, pour out on a single mom in your congregation. As you mentor her she will be greatly blessed, and so will you.

Gentlemen, beware. Single mothers can be in a desperate state. They may see your kindness and look to you as a provider rather than seeing Jesus. Ministering to this group by men should be done in a team setting only. Even if you feel that you are strong and would not give into temptation, you still need to keep all of those doors firmly closed. We are called to a higher standard than that of the world, and we need to avoid even the appearance of evil. Great ministries have fallen due to gossip as well as to real acts of sin.

Couples can minister together to single parent families very effectively. While the ladies enjoy some encouraging conversation over coffee the husband can offer to do some desperately needed household or vehicle repairs. A single mom often lacks the tools and the skills needed for day-to-day maintenance. Just by doing a little looking and asking we can do her and her children a real kindness.

We need to take this seriously. When we do not help those who are of the household of faith, the body suffers weakness in its parts. If one member suffers, we all suffer. We wonder why we do not have more revivals. This is an important key—we do not show kindness to those who are already in the household of faith. If we blessed and taught this precious saint to be a productive healthy part of the body, then the whole body would be more effective for outside ministry. As it is, we have broken body parts trying to function on their own.

In the early chapters of the book of Acts we see several examples of kindness by people helping one another giving to all who had need and organizing a daily distribution to the widows. We also see major revival. Thousands of people were saved. God loves to bless that kind of unity.

Now all who believed were together, and had all things in common, and sold their possessions and goods, and divided them among all, as anyone had need. So continuing daily with one accord in the temple, and breaking bread from house to house, they ate their food with gladness and simplicity of heart, praising God and having favor with all the people. And the Lord added to the church daily those who were being saved.

- Acts 2:44-47

We have gotten it all backwards. We try to do kindnesses to strangers and win them over to Jesus, kicking and screaming, one by one. God instructs us to do kindnesses to those who are believers, and when He sees that kind of unity, He will add to our numbers daily. When we look after the sheep He has already given to us he will add more to the flock using the Holy Ghost multiplication factor. He will bring them in by the thousands.

Why would He add to our numbers by the thousands if we are broken and defeated? That would just make many more broken and defeated Christians. That would be a great way to evangelize wouldn't it? We could say, "Come and join us, and then you can be miserable too!"

We have many needy people right in our congregations and communities. I do not mean to overlook any people group by focusing on single mothers. We can also visit and pray for the sick in hospitals, and help our elderly with practical applications of kindness. A pie can be baked for a neighbor, or meals can be prepared for a family in crisis. We need only to open our eyes, and the opportunities for kindness will abound.

Kindness is a sweet, exceptional fruit of the Holy Spirit, and it needs to be spread out over many areas. It is a liquid fruit, like the coconut milk that is used in skin care lotion. It softens the rough, dry spots of the body of Christ. It is a healing balm to the hurting around us and a refreshing drink in a hot dry world.

I pray right now that you will be more abundantly filled with the Holy Spirit, and that as a result He will pour into you the excellent fruit of kindness. May you look for opportunities to be a blessing to those around you, especially to those who are of the household of faith. I ask the Holy Ghost to pour out upon you abundant energy, so that you will not grow weary in doing good, but will be richly equipped for every good work. May the God of peace and love and kindness be with you in all that you do. I ask these things in the mighty Name of Jesus, praising Him and thanking Him, knowing that all that I ask for in His Name I shall receive.

Amen.

TWELVE

Self-control

Defeated. Miserable. Lonely. Anxious. Angry. Empty. Lustful. Out of control. Those were the poisonous, rotten fruits of my flesh that used to rule and reign in my body. Even though I called myself a Christian I was totally devoid of victory. The summary of the whole experience was in the words, "out of control." I felt powerless to change. I bought the lie that came straight from the pit. I thought that those characteristics were my lot in life. God must have made me that way. I could never change. I should accept the way that I was.

Today I thank God that he had a better plan. I praise Him for reaching down and pulling me out of the muck I had made for myself. When I finally came to the end of myself and gave it all to Jesus, everything changed. I realized that I was powerless. I was unable to change, so I asked God to change me, and gave Him my permission to take control and to use whatever means necessary to get the job done. I invited the Holy Spirit to take over, and He did.

He filled me right up and put me on overflow, and one of the fruit of that outpour has been the savory flavor of self-control.

The fabulous transformation that the Holy Ghost injected into my life in those early weeks was completed by self-control. Before, I had been so easy for the enemy to lure. I had several weaknesses that he had become accustomed to flaunting before my senses. Whenever I would become convicted of my sins, he would just increase the temptations. He knew just how to push my buttons. He would knock me off course by flattering me with praises and appealing to my pride. Mr. "Tall, Dark and Handsome" would show up at my door to appeal to my lust. The lottery tickets would arrive in the mail to appeal to my greed. Pre-approved credit cards enticed me to go a little more out of control.

Then the Holy Spirit moved in and took over control. Outpour brought with it the astounding ability to smell a rat at fifty paces. I was instantly aware in my spirit several chess moves ahead of the checkmate. I was empowered to back away and firmly close the door in the face of temptation. I had been radically set free.

The Holy Spirit taught me to see the temptation coming long before it ever got there. He showed me that it was not the final act of sin that had originally gotten me into trouble. My habits had fed my sin. For example, my sin of poor stewardship and over-spending did not start at the point of purchase. It started when I was feeling bored hours earlier, and decided to go down to "Mammon-mart" just to do some window worship. I was just going to look and not buy anything, but all that looking fed the greed within me, and my spirit was starved of all good food so it was powerless to defend itself. It did not take too long to succumb to the pressure and pull out my sacrificial offering (the credit card). There I would be, taking home my latest material fascination.

The Holy Spirit taught me to recognize that trap. He showed me that when I am making a purchase and I have an icky, ugly feeling in the pit of my stom-ach, that I should listen to that warning and put the item back. When I feel conviction I need to respond to it in obedience and pray, asking the Lord, "What would You have me do concerning this?"

As Christians, we need to recognize the doorways that lead to our sin. We need to close those door-ways long before we ever come to our weak point. I often share with young people that sexual sin does not begin with the final act. It begins with linger-ing looks and casual hand-holding. Kissing and touching have been designed by God to be the initial motivation that will lead to genetic multiplication. He made us that way so that as husbands and wives we would pro-create and populate the earth. If we do not want to go all the way, then we should not open the door at step one. If we keep our hands and our eyes pure then our bodies will have no choice but to follow.

It is not just young people that have trouble with lust. Our culture is permeated with it, and it is time that we as the church get real about it. Right in our pews, and even in our pulpits, people are struggling with temptations that war against our souls. We need to get transparent before one another and confess our weaknesses so that God can heal and deliver us out of that pit. Acting like there is no problem will not make it go away. Resisting the enemy causes him to flee, so we must actively resist him. We need to be filled to overflowing with the Holy Spirit in order to effectively combat this very real threat with the fruit of self-control.

I can speak with experience on this subject because I have been gloriously set free from the temptation of lust. Even though it is very humbling to speak of it, I must do so. The body of Christ has to face its weaknesses and submit them to our Lord. We need people who have been healed to stand up and encourage others. So, I confess to you my brothers and sisters that I have been released from the bondage of lust, and you can be as well. The Holy Spirit filled me up, and two amazing things began to happen.

First of all, I would get a check in my spirit whenever there was even a remote possibility that anyone might view a situation as inappropriate. At that point I would take a step back and ask God what He would like me to do. I may have felt Him leading me to end a conversation, or to invite another adult to join in.

Secondly, the Holy Spirit has poured out such a powerful anointing on me that men no longer view me as an object of interest. I have lost my sex appeal. Thank you Jesus! (Yes, I am rejoicing, for those of you who are not yet with me on this subject.)

People in general are attracted to me. All kinds of people of every age and both genders like to be around me, but it is no longer me that is drawing them to myself. It is definitely not good looks or charm. It is the light of Christ. He draws them to me, and as a result, they are affected for the gospel. It is really wonderful. It is much better than any of that old counterfeit attraction. I am so fulfilled in my role as an ambassador for Christ that I would not go back to that empty state of self-edification for anything. Jesus is so much better.

The Holy Spirit has also taught me how to resist the devil in my thoughts. Sometimes I would be going along minding my own business, when a totally ugly thought would enter into my head. It might be sexual, or greedy, or vengeful, but it was certainly not of the Lord. In the old days, I would have ignored it, or more likely I would have fed it and allowed it to dwell there. I would have continued to elaborate on the fantasy, but the Holy Spirit has since showed me that my thought life is important to God. He cares about my mind and He wants me to exercise the fruit of self-control even in my deepest, innermost thoughts.

> *...casting down arguments and every high thing that exalts itself against the knowledge of God, bringing every thought into captivity to the obedience of Christ...*
>
> *- 2 Corinthians 10:5*

Now when I have a nasty thought, I immediately confess it to God (out loud if possible so the devil knows he has been resisted), and then I rebuke that thought in the Name of Jesus. I usually quote the above Scripture over the incident, as well.

I have found in doing this that the devil does indeed flee when we resist him. Those thoughts have become fewer and fewer over time. I thank God for that freedom. Glory to His Holy Name!

There were other healthy side effects of growing the fruit of self-control. I was suddenly able to focus on the tasks at hand with total clarity. I no longer languished about in indecision. The aimlessness was gone, and I was able to complete projects for the first time in my life. I was also able to discern if I was not intended to start a project, and I was released to say no. I stopped making phony promises and my word started to mean what I said.

Self-control is not about being in control of ourselves—it is about giving up control to the Holy Spirit and allowing Him to rule and reign in our lives. He then fills us up to overflowing and pours out a wonderful fruit and by-product of deliverance called self-control. Suddenly we are released from bondages that have plagued us for all of our lives, and we are free to enjoy the fruit of self-control.

Self-control is like a kiwi. It is a sweet, juicy, little fruit that is no burden to bear. We can carry it in our pocket, and even the seeds are palatable. It is nice to have one around for a refreshing snack when there is an ugly temptation of a four fudge sundae trying to lure us over to the ice-cream bar. In our fruit salad, our kiwi of self-control adds just the right zip to the recipe. Mixed in with the rest it allows us to know when to bubble with joy and burst with love and show a little gentleness. Self-control is the perfect addition to the dish.

Heavenly Father, I praise You, God, and glorify You right now. I thank You, Lord, that You are continuing to pour out Your Holy Spirit into this precious saint's life. Lord, I ask You to give them a double helping of the fruit of self-control. May they be set free from bondages in their life and released to walk in the glorious fruit of self-control. May they give all control over to the Holy Spirit, and as a result exhibit tremendous self-control in the face of all temptation. Holy Spirit, I ask You to reveal to this person their weaknesses and the doorways that You would like to take control of. May You empower them for change and transformation, not by might, not by power, but by Your precious Spirit. In Jesus' Name I pray and ask these things.

Amen.

THIRTEEN

Humble Pie

*I*n some of the newer Bible translations kindness is listed as a fruit of the Spirit and meekness is left out. However, I have found that both kindness and humility have definitely grown on my own Spirit-filled tree. Therefore, I wanted to include this fruit as an encouragement to others.

Humility is not a popular character trait in our society. We have been taught to stand up for ourselves and to fight back. In some cases, we have even been instructed to get the other guy before he gets us. We talk about self-confidence being a good thing, and of self-awareness as being healthy. With all of the emphasis on self, however, where is our focus on God? What about God-confidence and God-awareness?

Was Jesus concerned with self-confidence the last night He spent with His disciples? No, He showed us humility by washing their feet only hours before He was going to die on the cross.

I used to not have any real understanding of humility, but it did start to grow on me when I was transformed. I did not notice it immediately, but I was no longer glory-hungry. I did not have to be the center of attention anymore. I no longer interrupted every conversation with my own better story or more fabulous idea. I no longer looked for my own picture first when I viewed a group photo.

Humility was growing on my tree in the background, rather small. It was bright enough to see if you looked hard for it amongst the other fruit. Humility is not as eye catching as apples nor as big as melons, and it is often not your first choice because it lacks sweetness. It is more like a lemon than any other fruit. We do not usually choose lemons to devour whole. We squeeze a little juice over our apples of love to keep them from turning brown or use it as a good cleaning agent. Like humility, they can be used to clean up a real big mess.

Sometimes, when we have been going along happily eating the fruit of cherries and mangoes, along comes a nasty situation and we have to take a great big bite of lemon. When we have to eat a whole pile of it, we cook those lemons into humble pie to make the dish more palatable.

Two years ago, when I moved into this community, I had all kinds of ideas for ministry projects. Imagine my shock when the Lord told me to shelve them all, and then to shut up and pray! I could not believe my ears. I asked Him, "But Lord, don't You know how talented I am?"

He knew. After all, it was God who had blessed me with all of those giftings. However, right then they were more of a problem than a blessing. I needed to learn to seek the giver and not the gift. I needed to make spending time with Him a priority, and I needed to learn to pray.

I thought that I knew how to pray. After all, I had cast out demons in the Name of the Lord. What more was there? I was really quite arrogant about it. I had learned humility in some ways but I had not even considered that it applied to my prayer time as well.

I thank God that He was patient with me and faithful to teach me. The Lord graciously put some good books into my hands on the subject of spiritual warfare, and I began to slowly realize that I hardly knew anything about prayer.

I had learned how to pray for my own needs quite well and I knew how to take authority in the Name of Jesus. However, I knew nothing about disciplined intercession, or the fact that time in prayer is time spent soaking in the presence of the Most High God.

The Holy Spirit led me on a journey through Nehemiah and Ezra. Then, as I began to develop a detailed prayer list, He taught me to pray the Word of God over it. He encouraged me to be faithful and not to pray only when I felt like it. Occasionally I would feel the presence of the Holy Spirit, but He showed me that I needed to pray even when I wasn't getting a goosepimply exciting rush from it. Sometimes, I was down right exhausted, and would even fall asleep praying, but God blessed those times too. The next morning I would awaken refreshed in my spirit and filled to overflowing, ready to face my busy day. God is really Awesome!

After two years of praying over that prayer list and seeing some fantastic results, I am so glad that the Holy Spirit took the time to teach me. Even though I was prideful and arrogant, He taught me to learn and to submit to His leading. Now, after all of that learning I know a lot more than I did before about praying. Most importantly, I know that I still do not know enough yet.

As the Lord has humbled me in my prayer habits, He has humbled me greatly in other areas as well. He has laid it on my heart to go back and make restitution to people that I hurt before I was changed. That has been a very humbling enterprise. I did not realize how many people there were until I started facing up to them. I am still regularly writing letters to people from my past as the Lord brings the events to my memory. (So, if you are one of those people and you have not received yours yet, it will likely be in the mail soon.)

However, the acts of humility that are the hardest to handle are the ones that come up in our day-to-day lives. They are the experiences where six things went wrong before lunch and now here is one more nasty individual standing right in our face raining on our parade.

These are the times we want to stand up and fight back. We want to holler and scream and stomp our feet. We yell, "It's not fair!" or, "Don't you dare talk to ME like that!"

In the old days I was a real yeller. I wrote letters to the editor about injustices. I probably would have marched in parades, but small towns did not have any. I used to get into a person's space over any little beef that I had, but God has used several experiences to purge that tendency right out of me.

The next couple of stories that I am going to share with you are of a very personal nature. I want you to understand that even now as I write them I am being deeply humbled once again. I am not telling these stories to gain your sympathy or so you will think that I am some great person. I am not.

I am going to share these stories with the world for two reasons. First of all, I want you to realize that you, too, can be humble. It may hurt a little at the time, but it will be well worth it in growth. These types of experiences will release you very effectively from any bondages of pride. Secondly, I share these accounts so that it will glorify my Father in heaven. I ask you to remember what I was like before the work of transformation that the Holy Spirit has done in me. He will do it in you, too, if you will let Him.

A few years ago I helped a single mother move into the community that I lived in. I promoted her cause to other Christians, and together we helped get her out of a situation involving alcohol and abuse. Over the next five months I watched her blossom right before my eyes. She read her Bible, hungrily devouring the Word of God. We had many Bible studies, afternoon coffees, and late night conversations. Her children got saved and began to be transformed as well. They improved in their schoolwork, and they began to show more obvious signs of respect for their mother. I loved her and her children very deeply, and they were a real blessing to me.

Then, while I was away for a two-week vacation, my friend fell into temptation. She had been feeding her spirit, but she was young in the faith and had come from an extremely burdened past. Those old bondages came back to haunt her, and she gave in. Well-meaning family members who wanted her closer to themselves loaded her up and moved her back in with her abusive boyfriend.

When I returned I went to her home and discovered that she was gone. I felt terrible enough about that, but to make matters worse I found out from her neighbor that she had left without paying the rent. Gossip was rapidly spreading through our little town that she had been somebody who used people, and that I had taught her how to do it. They were saying that I had talked people into giving her things. They said that I had taken her to local help agencies and showed her how to get more stuff.

I was grieved by losing my friend, and now, on top of it all, I had to put up with the devil's lies, too. He is so crooked, and he always perverts the facts to his own ends. There were small elements of truth in each tale, but they were greatly embellished and badly exaggerated. I had taken her to different places and people during those five months, but she had never lied. She really was a single mother who had come from desperate circumstances, and she legitimately needed help. No matter what happened, I would not have traded those five months for anything. I know that she was blessed and that those children were blessed as a result. They will remember the love that was sown into them for the rest of their days, and God's Word will not return to Him void. There was precious seed sown into that precious family, and I am glad for the opportunity to have known them. I love them still, and am not idle in my prayers concerning them.

Regarding the gossip, I laid it before God and asked Him what He would have me do about it. He showed me something that I will never forget. He showed me to refrain from justifying myself in any of it.

You see, I could have gone to person after person, but I would never have been able to stamp it all out. The harder I tried, the more they would gossip. My talking about it to the people who gossiped would only fuel the fire.

So, the Lord showed me to do something very odd indeed. It was also very humbling. At the time I did not realize it, but it was going to be completely effective to eliminate all of the gossip.

The Holy Spirit told me to go and pay her bill.

Oh, I argued with Him. I still have enough of the

flesh in me to put up an argument. It was a lot of money, and a real sacrifice for me. I told God that it was not my bill. Then He reminded me that I had talked her landlord into trusting her in the first place. I must have said "But Lord...." about six times, but it finally came down to one question: "Am I really going to serve Jesus or not?"

In the end, I bit off a great big chunk of bitter, sour humble pie, and took an envelope of money over to her landlord. I did not know it, but my Lord was about to do a miracle.

Unbeknownst to me, this man was also a talker. He had probably had not one good thing to say about me or my friend up to that point. But when I came over with an apology and the restitution to back it up, he did a double take! He was visibly overwhelmed as I gave it to him, and then he went out and said very nice things about us all over town. The gossip ended. The devil had tried to use that situation to defame my friend and to discredit my ministry, but God turned it all around to His glory. Thank You, Jesus!

That landlord has a very different opinion of Christians today than what he used to, and he shares his opinion a lot. Praise the Lord!

Since that time the Lord has taught me that humility is a powerful weapon of spiritual warfare. It softens people's hearts toward the gospel and toward the servants of the Lord. He has told me to apologize for things that I did not do, pay for things that I did not damage, and give the credit to Him or to others whenever possible. He has instructed me to repent on behalf of sinners, and to quickly accept responsibility for my own sin. I have eaten so much humble pie that I have acquired a taste for it. Glory to God!

When I gave my life totally to Jesus, I gave up my right to be offended. When someone persecutes me they are persecuting my Lord, and it is His offense not mine. When I remember that and act out of humility, it glorifies Him. However, when I overreact in offence, it steals glory from Him.

So, am I perfect now?

No. Far from it. Sadly, I still make mistakes and get into the flesh from time to time. But the good news is that I do it very seldom, and when I do, I repent very quickly.

Just a couple of weeks ago Jesus gave me another opportunity to eat some humble pie. I was confronted once again with a landlord on my step. Unfortunately, I forgot everything I ever learned in Sunday school and soundly told him off. But it only took a couple of hours for the Holy Spirit to straighten me out, and I had to go humbly apologize before suppertime. I praise God that He dealt with me quickly.

Occasionally we have a tremendous opportunity to glorify God with the fruit of humility. It may be a situation where we may be right to blow our top, but no matter how right we are to sound off, or how justly deserved it might be, it will not lead that person to Jesus. Nor will it influence them to move in favor for one of God's people. Humility will win them to Christ. It is a fruit that points to Him. There is no worldly explanation for our behavior and so it makes the unbeliever sit up and ask, "What was that?"

Dear Lord, I lift up the reader right now to You and ask for even more of Your precious Holy Spirit to be poured out into their life. May You give them a special blessing of the fruit of humility. May You empower them to apologize and to make restitution for past situations. May You strengthen them to respond to day-to-day events in a humble manner that glorifies You. Lord, when they fall, as we all do, may You cause them to repent quickly, and call out to You for forgiveness. In the Name of Jesus I pray. Amen.

FOURTEEN

Weeds In The Orchard

As saints, we have been seeded into the garden of God to grow a crop that produces a hundredfold. The light of Christ should shine in us in such a way that it glorifies God and draws sinners to us. They should see victory in our personal lives as we display peace in the midst of chaos, and joy in the middle of trial. The fruit of the Holy Ghost should be plentiful, colorful, and appealing to the eye of the unsaved.

In the previous chapters, I have shared testimonies of how the continual filling of the Holy Spirit has brought forth much juicy fruit in my own life. I have poured out to you the difference Jesus has made as I have given Him complete control.

It is my deepest desire to see others transformed by the power and the presence of the Holy Spirit. That way they, too, can live their lives on fire for Jesus, set free and victorious. For this reason I am going to share with you a few attitudes that may be holding you back, and also show you how you can deal with them in order to experience total freedom.

Just before I was powerfully filled with the Holy Spirit I had a period of deep repentance before my Lord. I had to get right with Him and I had to get real with Him. If I had continued to go my own way, I would not have been so radically transformed and set free. As long as I was comfortable with my sin there was no hope for change.

WEED #1 COMPLACENCY

If we really want to change our circumstances or our attitudes, we need to get uncomfortable in our rut. If we do not like where we are right now, then we have to stop doing the things that got us there.

In our personal habits, we have to face our complacency. We have to stop believing the enemy's lies about us. He tells us that we are never going to change, that this is the way we have always been, and that this is the way that we will always be.

If God had made us in such a way that we could not change, He would not have commanded us to be transformed.

And do not be conformed to this world, but be transformed by the renewing of your mind, that you may prove what is that good and acceptable and perfect will of God.

— *Romans 12:2*

Complacency is not a friend of the church. It is a tool of Satan. He uses it to get us very comfortable in our circle so that we will not venture out to claim more of the land for Jesus. He makes praying and evangelism seem like too much work. He tells us we should just send some money overseas and enjoy the good life. Let the pastor invite people to church, that is his job. We do not want to get too much joy happening lest we look fanatical. It is nice to go to a church where the program is predictable, and it is very comfortable.

Tradition in a church is nice if it is Scriptural. However, if it is just tradition, then it is just another one of the ways of man. Tradition does not usually get people saved, healed and delivered. If a church has only seen ten people saved in ten years, then perhaps it is time to throw out the tradition and pray for the Holy Ghost to have His way.

God likes us to be on fire for Him. He is not impressed by apathy and complacency. Our material wealth is of little value to Him who owns all things. He wants us to hunger and thirst for Him like a deer panting for water. He wants us to display a heated passion as we serve Him. No matter how much we own, if we lack that on fire passion for Him, He sees us as poor and wretched. It grieves Him and it sickens Him. Lukewarm Christians make Him vomit.

"I know your works, that you are neither cold nor hot. I could wish you were cold or hot. So then, because you are lukewarm, and neither cold nor hot, I will vomit you out of My mouth. Because you say, 'I am rich, have become wealthy, and have need of nothing' — and do not know that you are wretched, miserable, poor, blind, and naked — I counsel you to buy from Me gold refined in the fire, that you may be rich; and white garments, that you may be clothed, that the shame of your nakedness may not be revealed; and anoint your eyes with eye salve, that you may see. As many as I love, I rebuke and chasten. Therefore be zealous and repent."

- Revelation 3:15-19

Our Father loves us. He says this out of love for us. We can have so much more than what we have right now if we will just listen.

We do not need more money—we need more of Jesus. When Jesus needed to pay his taxes, he got the money out of a fish. He fed 5000 people with five loaves of bread and a few fish. He did not lack. Neither will we, if we put Him first in our lives... if we will learn to follow Him as He leads us.

Was Jesus lukewarm? Was He worried about comfort? Did he take long vacations in beautiful places, throwing a few nickels to the poor as He went? Did He have a cozy retirement fund? (This is getting kind of uncomfortable isn't it?)

Jesus loves us, but material blessings like these are not the things that bring us lasting joy. Lasting joy comes from the Holy Spirit. It is one of the fruit that grows on the tree of the Holy Ghost-filled believer.

WEED #2 REBELLION

Rebellion is choosing our own way over the way of God. "My way is better than God's way," is what we are saying. This makes us out to be smarter than God. It is a form of idol worship as we serve the god of self. This is why Our Father sees this as witchcraft, and He will not lift us up to a place of victory as a result.

"For rebellion is as the sin of witch-craft, And stubbornness is as iniquity and idolatry, Because you have reject-ed the word of the Lord, He also has rejected you from being king."
- *1 Samuel 15:23*

Saul had been rebellious and had not humbled himself before the Lord. He figured that God had anointed him, so he did not need to wait for the prophet to come and offer the sacrifice. But God will not exalt those who exalt themselves. As Saul was removed from leadership, so will we be if we refuse to humble ourselves and become obedient to God's will in our lives. If we refuse to be continually filled with the Holy Spirit, we will not bear good fruit that draws others to us. Our own rebellious choices will cause us to continue living in defeat.

WEED #3 FOOLISHNESS

Throughout the book of Proverbs there is much teaching on foolishness. It may not be a popular sub-ject in our Christian circles, but if it were not impor-tant, God would not have spent so much time on it. Many people lack victory in their lives because they believe they have already arrived, and they are satis-fied with the crumbs from the banquet table. They are already very knowledgeable. They have a measure of peace and prosperity, so they are quite comfortable. They have a measure of victory over sin, so they keep their little bad habits, the small white lies, the broken promises and the perverted thoughts. These are hidden things; they look all cleaned up on the outside so they do not feel any pressure to clean up the inside.

God sees everything. His eyes miss nothing. He knows the attitudes of our hearts. He sees bigotry, He sees lust, and He sees selfishness and self-righteousness. Nothing is missed. He defines foolishness as our unwillingness to accept correction and change as a result. If we already have all of the answers then we are impossible to teach.

If we are lacking in peace when we go to sleep at night, or reacting in anger with those that we love, then it is time to face foolishness head-on.

Accept the rebuke of the Lord. If you are so right, then why are you so miserable? There is no peace in following our own ways. Give these areas over to Him. Ask Jesus for the power to change as you submit your will to Him. When He tells you to do something in His Word, do not argue with Him. Be obedient and let Him bless you in it.

Ask God to fill you with His Holy Spirit and submit every area of your life to His leading—even the areas that you think that you already know everything about.

WEED #4 PRIDE

Pride is a big ugly weed that sneaks up real fast and eats you like a Venus Fly Trap with legs. We can be legitimately serving the Lord, going along minding our own business, and along comes the voice of flattery. It can come with a slight mocking sarcasm, or it may come from a subtler source such as a lukewarm Christian. "You are working sooo hard," it may say, or, "You are such a good leader, sooo talented."

Practicing humility is good way to dig that weed out of the garden. Ask the Lord for more of His Spirit and practice humility by immediately passing all credit on to Jesus. We must not be too eager to validate our ministries or ourselves. When we have been anointed by God for a certain task, He will exalt us in due season as we submit to His leading. We must remember that Jesus got people to follow Him by being a good servant, not by being a military dictator. This is true in our homes and our workplaces, as well as in our congregations.

Doing menial tasks for others is a fabulous way to root out this monster weed. Apologizing first is like dumping poison on its roots. Praying for those who persecute you starves it out. Pride weeds do not last long around Christians who are submitted to the promptings of the Holy Spirit and filled to overflowing by His presence.

WEED #5 NOT COMING
UNDER AUTHORITY

This is a prickly, dry type of weed that causes a believer to stand alone. It reminds me of a huge cactus out in the desert. "I do not need other Christians to fellowship with," it says. "I have been hurt by churches." This one really likes to talk about the bad things that have happened to it. These may even all be truthful incidences, but it ignores that, as Christians, we are to lay aside our offences. We no longer have a right to be offended. We gave that right to Jesus.

Unity is definitely God's idea. The first four chapters of Acts are all about unity. Because of that unity God moved, and people got saved, healed and set free by the thousands. There is no unity in standing alone. By ourselves we cannot lead people to Jesus by the tens, never mind the thousands.

This weed will go after really talented Christians and try to isolate them from the body of Christ to keep them ineffective for the kingdom of God. They claim that they get their authority directly from the Lord and do not need to be submitted to any man. That sounds very nice, however it is not Scriptural.

God likes mentorship. He is big into accountability. Barnabas mentored Paul, Elisha had Elijah, and even Moses spent forty years in training on the backside of the desert with Jethro, the high priest of Midian.

What about Jesus? Yes, that's a good question.
Now I have one for you. What was He doing when
He went to John the Baptist to be baptized? This
was a public act of submission to an established
ministry. Later, He also took some of John's disciples into his ministry when they lost their leader.
Submission to one another is God's idea. If we will
not submit to men that we can see, how will we submit to God who we see by faith?

The best way to expose this weed is to look at its
fruit.   Quite simply—hurting people hurt others.
Free people are used by God to set others free. If
people are being transformed and saved, and if God
is being abundantly glorified, this is good fruit.
However, if you are a Christian who feels that you
do not need to come under authority and you are not
experiencing love, joy, and peace in Biblical propor-
tions - GIVE IT UP! God will not change His Word
for any one person. It stands for eternity. Any person who encourages you not to fellowship in a body
of Christians is just telling you what your itching
ears want to hear.

I could have fallen into this trap so easily myself.
I thank God that He saw a way for me to avoid it.
Early in those days after I was transformed the
Lord began to use me to lay my hands on the sick
and to cast out demons. It would have been so easy
to get prideful and not come under authority. After
all, I was doing something that many pastors were
not doing. I could have used that as an excuse. I
could have said that I knew more than they did, so
why should I submit to their leadership?

Fortunately, the Lord had provided me with a wise and mighty man of God as the pastor of the church that I attended. The Holy Spirit impressed me to go to this man to tell him the things that I was doing and to submit to him. I thank God for that pastor even today. He did not discourage me and he did not quench the Spirit. He wisely offered an open door and discipleship. He saw the transformation in me and recognized the work of the Holy Ghost.

Some people get filled up with the Holy Spirit, manifest various gifts and fruit, and then go to their home churches the next Sunday all excited and bubbling everywhere. Their leadership may have never seen such an expression of manifest joy, and out of ignorance or caution may react negatively.

What should these people do? Run away?

This is a very sticky situation, but fortunately we are not lost without the guidance of the Holy Spirit. The first thing that needs to be done is to put it to prayer. Ask God where He would like you to be planted for long-term growth. While you wait on Him, continue to go to your church and be a light there as long as you can. There will come a point however, where you will no longer be able to sow into that situation. Sometimes your church may even move to dis-fellowship you. Do not despair, you are not being dis-fellowshipped from God, only from some of His people who are not yet willing for Him to have His way in their midst. Wait upon the Lord and He will direct you to where He is calling you.

Do not take offence. The devil can use this situation if you are not careful. He will try to make you feel rejected, but you have given up the right to be offended. It is not God's will that you separate yourself indefinitely from all of His people. He knows just the right place for you to grow and be released to your personal calling.

Do not try to justify yourself to your old congregation, or to validate your ministry to those who do not understand. When we humble ourselves before God and honestly seek His will, He will exalt us in due season. Many times when a person gets filled up with the Holy Ghost they are rejected from lukewarm, or traditional fellowship, but years later those same people will acknowledge the good fruit that has grown on that tree. Even if they do not, we have to live our lives to please God, not people.

If you have concerns about leaving a church that you have attended since childhood, just pray about it and ask God to lead you. It is very important to feed your spirit and to grow in the things of God. If you do not go to a church where the Spirit of God is moving, you will not be growing, and those who are not filled with the Holy Spirit will suck the life right out of you. They are bound in tradition, habits and religious rules that do not lead the lost to Christ or set people free. Jesus wants to use you to lead others to Christ. If you have been unsuccessful doing this where you have been going, then perhaps you need some deeper teaching.

Pray about it. If there has been a change in leadership at your church or a change in attitude toward the Holy Spirit, then pray for your church and seek God's face concerning where He wants you to be. Be sensitive to the Holy Spirit and look to Him for direction.

As you grow your fruit will grow, and it may yet cause some of your old friends to acknowledge that God has done something wonderful in you. They may even seek that transformation out for themselves. However, if you stay where you have always been, and do what you have always done, you will get what you always got. God wants us to keep growing in His Word and to be continually transformed into being more like Jesus.

The Lord has a place for you to fellowship all picked out for you. Seek Him for that direction, and once you have allowed Him to guide you there, also allow Him to plant you there. You will not always agree with the pastor. He is just a man after all, and not perfect. You may have conflicts from time to time with members of the body. However, we are not called to argue and disagree. We are called to pray for those in leadership. Ask God to intervene so that His Word is taught and He is worshiped the way that He wants to be worshiped. Pray for strength and wisdom for your pastor. Plead the blood of Jesus over him or her and their family, and stand in the gap for unity in their home. It is not easy being a pastor. Ask the Lord to fill him or her with more of the Holy Spirit.

We need to find a place where we can grow, but there is no perfect congregation. If we are looking for the perfect church to attend, we will not find it.

Churches are filled with imperfect people and we ourselves mess things up sometimes. We are called to be a forgiving people who love the unlovable. We can come up with excuses to stay away from church all day long, but they are just excuses. Let's just give in to the Holy Spirit and ask for more of Him in our lives. Then good fruit will flow from us and we will all get along together beautifully.

WEED #6 DEMONS

When a believer has trouble going into a church that is flowing in the Holy Ghost, I find that interesting. If they shake, cry, or suddenly feel ill, I am even more interested. When they experience panic attacks, arguments in the parking lot with their spouse, or even vomiting; it is very likely there is something going on there.

Have trouble reading or understanding your Bible? How about ringing in your ears, or sudden tiredness during a sermon that you need to hear? If the ideas of deliverance, the blood of Jesus, or the Holy Ghost cause fear or anxiety to well up in you, it is very likely that you are experiencing a demonic manifestation.

"Oh, but I am a Christian," you may say. "I could not possibly have a demon!"

Let's lay all of the theological jargon aside right now. I was a lukewarm Christian, and I was definitely demonized. After I was set free, one of the first deliverances that God used me in was a traveling evangelist from Brazil. The man was a walking salvation machine. I never saw anyone more dedicated. He would run up to people in the street, sharing his testimony and handing out tracts wherever he went. He spoke in tongues, but he lacked victory in some major fruit areas. So, we laid hands on him in the Name of Jesus, and the demon actually spoke out of his mouth and tried to use the man's body to strike us down!

Christians can definitely have demons. It is a great place for them to hide—right where nobody would suspect to look.

I am not going to debate whether they are in your spirit or in your soul? Are they in you, around you, or on your left ear lobe? If they are anywhere near you, get rid of them! If you have received the Holy Spirit they do not possess your spirit, however they can still harass or oppress you. They can still manifest in outward habits and cause a loss of productivity in your life.

Just spending time on the front row of a really anointed meeting will cause many of them to flee. However, if you have already been doing this and are still not seeing change and transformation, seek out deliverance.

Find a Spirit-filled pastor or lay person who is under the authority of a church and is accountable to others. Make sure that it is someone who has a track record of success. You are also looking for someone who can get the job done in 3 to 4 sessions, maximum. It should not take five years of counseling to do deliverance. This person of God should lay hands on you in the Name of Jesus and deal with whatever you have going on.

Demons can come into a person through four different ways:

First of all, if we willfully choose to sin, we open up a doorway to the demonic. They love rebellion.

Secondly, occult activity is another wide open door. Ouija boards, yoga, martial arts, hypnotism, astrology and the Masonic lodge are just a few of their favorite entry points.

Thirdly, they jump on trauma victims. Wherever there is great fear there is no faith, and demons can move on in if they happen to be around. Accidents, fires, rape, incest, murder or anything traumatic can allow a demon to transfer.

Last of all, there are generational curses to consider. Alcoholism, wife battering, drug abuse, pedophilia, perversions and various hereditary ailments are some demonic elements that can be passed on to the next generation.

The good news is that speaking the Name of Jesus over them can effectively eliminate these things.

Do not discount what I am saying.

Much of Jesus' ministry was casting out demons. Do you think they all went away 2000 years ago? We just have new names for old problems. If you need deliverance, seek it out and get it over with.

Learn to take authority in the Name of Jesus and ask God to fill you with more of Himself. More of

Him is all that we need. More of His Holy Spirit. More, more, more.

Throughout this book I have prayed over you that you would be filled, filled, filled to overflowing. Now it is your turn. Get out a pen and a paper and look over the weeds. Write down the areas that you need to submit to God. Write down anything else that you need to yield as well and then pray and give each one to Jesus. Lay them down at the foot of the cross and tell Him that you are backing away and not picking them up again. Pray it out loud so that the enemy also knows that he has lost that hold on your life.

Then ask God for more of His Spirit. Ask Him to fill every void to overflowing. Cry out for more of His presence. Ask for more of Him in the Name of Jesus.

Ask and you shall receive.

FIFTEEN

My Cup Overfloweth

Throughout the Bible there are many references to the spirit of man. We have a spirit. It is that part of us that lives on when our body perishes. It is that part of us that communes with God. Before we get saved we do not exercise our spirit much. We are hardly conscious of it, but when we come to know the Lord and receive His Spirit, our spirit becomes alive within us.

The Spirit Himself bears witness with our spirit that we are children of God...
- Romans 8:16

Let us imagine that our spirits are like large empty wine glasses. When we receive the Holy Spirit a delightful splash of delicious deep red grape juice is immediately poured in. Now there is about an inch of bright purplish liquid in the bottom of the glass.

Perhaps this experience happens at church, and perhaps we leave there that Sunday feeling all warm and fuzzy like something wonderful has just happened. We go home, and over the next couple of days that yummy feeling dissipates somewhat. Then Tuesday evening we have a nasty argument with our spouse over some silly little thing. What happens to the cup? Does it go down? We can get theological at this point and say, "Well, the Holy Spirit that you received on Sunday night is always with you." Well, we know that He is with us. We still have assurance of salvation, and we have assurance that we have received the Holy Spirit. But we also know that God wants to give us more of His Spirit, so He has given us an inner sensor system called emotions that can give us some warnings when our spirit cup is getting low. Now, we are not to let our emotions rule over us. This is not an excuse to act miserable because our cup is empty. But we can react to those feelings and feed our spirit accordingly. If we are starting to feel icky and ugly then let's do something about it.

Praise the Lord, Wednesday at lunchtime you have an afternoon Bible Study and you are feeling better again. The cup is half full. That night you attend midweek services and the presence of the Holy Spirit is rapturous and your cup is now almost full.

Thursday is uneventful, so out of boredom you watch television for three hours. Two programs were not really that bad, and the cup stayed the same. Nothing went in, and nothing came out. However, program number three is laden with sex, violence and witchcraft. You go to bed that night feeling like you need a bath, and your cup is down to that inch in the bottom again.

Friday morning you get up and argue with the kids as they get ready for school. An afternoon meeting that you were looking forward to cancels. On the way home from work you pick up the mail and realize that your spouse put a large sum of money on one of the credit cards. How does your cup look now?

Our spirits are like empty vessels. They need to be continually filled with the Holy Spirit to be in that constant position of overflow. If we are not on over-flow, we react out of the flesh instead of the Spirit because our spirit is dry and there is nothing left in it. We get angry, we swear, and we kick the dog.

Everything that we do is either feeding our spirit, feeding our flesh, or wasting time until we feed our spirit or our flesh. Some activities, like listening to music without words, may not suck anything out of the cup, but they do not put anything in either.

There are several things that drain our spirits, like sinful activities, music that does not glorify

Jesus and evil television programs. Arguments and confrontations can also take a lot out of us.

There are also several things that feed our spirits. These things, when they are done with consistency, will put us into a place of continual overflow. These activities feed our spirits and encourage the presence of the Holy Spirit. As the Holy Spirit pours into us, our cup overflows all over everyone and everything that we touch. Our cup runs over, and good, delicious, juicy fruit abounds.

READING THE WORD

Pray that God gives you an appetite and a zeal for His Word. Spend time reading the Scripture on your own every day. If time is a problem, start out with five minutes before you fall asleep. Try some proverbs or some psalms. They are packed with lots of God's wisdom and they can be swallowed in small sittings. Then, as time goes on, work your way up to reading a book of the Bible. Luke, John and Acts are wonderful to start with.

Reading the Word can be an enjoyable experience that sows the Word into our spirits, and shows us our Father's love and plan for us. It is a time of learning and growing. It does not have to be a lot of time. We do not want it to be another form of bondage, where we have to read so many hours a day to achieve a quota. It is better to read a small amount that we understand well and think about, than it is to read whole books of the Bible and forget.

Joining a weekly Bible study class can be a lot of fun, and you can learn a lot about the Scripture as you study in a small group. You will be encouraged, stimulated and uplifted by the fellowship, as well.

MEDITATE ON THE WORD

Meditation on God's Word is different then reading. It is also different than new age transmeditation. Do not clear your mind of all thoughts. The devil can do a lot with an empty mind.

Meditating on God's Word means to focus on it and to study it. In Hebrew, the definitions of meditation are broad. They include: to repeat, to imagine, to think about, to declare, to pray and to speak. Meditation causes the Word to become a part of our spirit, not just our memory. The Word becomes alive to us and real for our own life situation.

When I first learned to meditate on God's Word I would take one Scripture and write it out on a 3 x 5 card. I would read it out loud several times a day over the length of a week. Once I had committed it to my memory, I would ask myself questions about it, like, "What is God trying to tell me personally through this Scripture?" or, "How does this apply to me?" Sometimes I would look up key words in the Hebrew or Greek language for greater clarification. After I felt that I had a good understanding, I would move on to another verse.

It was after about the third week of this that the Holy Spirit began to wake me up in the middle of

the night for special time with Him. I highly recommend meditation on the Word of God!

PRAISING THE LORD

Praising the Lord is pleasing to Him. He loves to
draw near to us as we declare His glory. We can
come right into His presence while we are in our
bedroom at night, in our kitchen washing the dishes in the morning, or even in a large crowd at a
church gathering.

Learn some praise songs by heart and sing whenever you can. Do not worry about how your voice
sounds. God is not concerned if we are scratchy or
even off key. He just loves to hear us sing to Him.

Make songs up about how you love Him, sing a
Psalm, or sing in tongues if you have that gifting.
Learn to enter into worship no matter where you
are or what you are doing.

I have never been a morning person. Sometimes
I can get almost ugly when I'm half asleep cleaning
the fifth spill off the floor and picking cheerios off
the bottom of my slippers. But if I can work up a
song, the evil mood melts away. If I cannot get one
going, I thank God for excellent praise music on
CD's!

Praise and worship is also a fabulous method of
spiritual warfare. Remember when Paul and Silas
were beaten and thrown into prison, and they
began to sing unto the Lord praising Him? God
moved heaven and earth and they were set physically free.

Once, when I was in an overwhelming financial crisis, I made my requests known unto God and then spent a few hours on my face praising Him and worshiping Him. By the following morning, God had moved heaven and earth on my behalf, and He will do the same for you as well.

PRAYER

Prayer is not just a time to ask God to do things for us. It is a time of sitting in His presence, soaking in the anointing of the Holy Spirit. There are several ways to pray that are both pleasing to God and nourishing to our spirit. We can pray on our knees, lay prostrate on the floor or walk around with our hands in the air. We can fast and pray alone, or be part of a congregational prayer chain. Any of these are fantastic.

However, when the Lord really began to deal with me on the subject of prayer He showed me two more methods that I had not considered.

1. Praying the Word

God's Word is true and it is definitely His will. There is nothing that He would rather answer than His own Word, so learn to pray it.

Whatever the circumstance is, you can find a segment of Scripture that covers the need, and speak it out loud over your life. Always start by praising Him, and then lead right into it something like this:

Heavenly Father, I praise You and glorify Your
Holy Name for You are awesome and worthy to be
praised. Thank You Jesus for this day. You are
mighty and I exalt You above all else.

Father God, I ask that You would cause me to do all
things without complaining and disputing, that I
would become blameless and harmless, a child of God
without fault in the midst of a crooked and perverse
generation. Cause me to shine as a light in this world.
In Jesus' Name, Amen.

The above is a Scripture modified for prayer from
Philippians 2:14-15.

We can also pray and declare the Word of God
over our situations in faith. We can say it as though
we already have it and thank our Lord for it as we
go. These prayers are powerful over every aspect of
our lives. I frequently pray this way for more wisdom, finances or health.

We can also sing the Word as we worship God; this
is an extremely high form of praise that can be
enjoyed by men as well as angels. Glory to His Name!

2. Intercession

Intercession is praying for others. We can learn
a lot by making a prayer list and disciplining ourselves to pray over our families, our communities
and any other projects or missionaries that the Lord
lays on our hearts.

I highly recommend making a prayer list that is
different for each night of the week. Do not put too

many items on each night or it will be too overwhelming. If you miss one night, you can make it up the next night, but do not try to do more than two lists in one night. When you fall off the wagon, just let it go, and start all over again right where you are. Keep up this practice for a year and you will see answered prayer as well as miracles in yourself as you continue to grow.

During intercession you can also declare and pray the Word of God over others. It is a wonderful practice that brings heavenly results. Praise the Lord!

FELLOWSHIP

Going to a Spirit-filled church does feed your spirit, but it is not enough. God wants more of your time and your heart than just two hours on Sunday morning. Try a weekly meeting as well, and look for special events to attend that the Holy Ghost is going to be moving in.

Also, look for mentors that will uplift you, encourage you, and even ground you. I used to get so excited with all that God was doing. However, we do not want to get so heavenly minded that we are no earthly good. God has put some very special people into my life to keep my feet on the ground while my eyes are focused on heaven.

We need buddies that are at our level to grow with, and we need mentors who know more than we do to be accountable to. A good mix of both is healthy for our spirit.

In all of this fellowship, do not overlook training as well. Attend conferences and seminars whenever possible. If you are married, put special priority on a couple's retreat at least once a year. Also watch for problematic areas in your life that could be strengthened with some focused teaching. This will give you a lot of nourishment for your spirit and fill your cup with that extra overflow, ready for when the need arises.

BOOKS, TAPES, AND VIDEOS

Holy Ghost infilling on the move! In our portable "drive–through" society, learn to put music and training tapes in the car. Feed your spirit by listening to your favorite evangelist while you clean your house. (I call it anointed house cleaning!) Watch a video while you fold clothes or take ten minutes to dance around the living room to a favorite CD with your toddlers. They will love it and so will you!

Take a good book along in your purse or carry a mini Bible in your back pocket. Read it when you are standing in line or waiting in your car. Not only does it feed your spirit but it also opens doors to sharing the gospel.

Give. Give. Give. Whatever you sow is what you shall reap. I used to hoard my books and loan them out, always hanging in the balance waiting for their return. But praise the Lord! God brought me Russ and Lorraine, a wonderful Christian couple, when I was only 18 years old. They tried to help me become successful in a multi-level business, but unfortunately, I was still too messed up to achieve victory at that time. They loved me anyway, and have continued to give to me liberally over the years. They sowed seeds of love into me through books, tapes, and videos that caused me to grow in spite of myself. Over the years their encouragement was always an example as they continued to draw me back to the Lord through their love. Today I find that the lessons that they taught me in business also work well in the sharing of the gospel.

When we sow bountifully we will also reap bountifully. When I learned to give books and videos away by the dozens, people started giving them to me by the hundreds. As a result, I now have a library in my bedroom, and I am abundantly blessed to be a blessing to others. Thank You, Jesus. Praise the Lord!

ACCEPTING YOUR CALLING

Many people have an anointed talent from God. When they use that particular gifting, there is a blessing that flows out. It affects those around them, and the person with the skill is also blessed as they are used by God to minister to others. They may receive abundant energy or a great sense of fulfillment as the anointing of the Holy Spirit falls on them.

I can be dead-tired and ready to drop, but give me an opportunity to preach and the anointing is instantly all over me. Suddenly I am alive and on fire for Jesus.

Some people are painters, writers, musicians, singers or sculptors. Some are blessed with gifts of helps, hospitality or administration. Some are anointed in their occupation to do excellent work that shows the light of Jesus in their lives. Whatever your personal gifting is, learn to flow in it, and use it to glorify the Lord. As you do so, He will pour forth His Spirit to anoint the work of your hands and to draw unbelievers to you as a result. As you give, you will also receive. Glory to God!

THE GIFTS OF THE SPIRIT

The gifts of the Spirit are given by God to bring glory to His Name. If we serve Jesus then we need to obediently accept all that He wants to give to us. He desires to give us more of the Spirit so that we can display a bountiful harvest of excellent, juicy fruit, and so that we will be empowered by His gifts to minister to others and serve Him better. There is an element of the enemy that circulates amongst the saints causing some to despise too much of the Holy Spirit. Do not fear exposure to the Holy Ghost, and do not avoid it. God knows how to give good gifts to His children. He would not give them to us if they were not good for us and those around us.

Some would have us believe that God stopped giving these gifts when the twelve original apostles died. There is no Scriptural evidence to support this, and much more experiential evidence proves that this is simply not so. Scripturally, there is much teaching on the gifts and their proper use and function in the body. Yes, there are gifts. Yes, they are for now as well as for 2000 years ago. God does not change.

Jesus Christ is the same yesterday, today, and forever.

- Hebrews 13:8

If our Lord gave gifts during His ministry on earth when He walked right here among us, would it not make sense that we would continue to need them later on, as well? Yes, God still raises up apostles, prophets, teachers, pastors and evangelists. Our need for them continues, and He is faithful to meet that need.

And He Himself gave some to be apostles, some prophets, some evangelists, and some pastors and teachers, for the equipping of the saints for the work of the ministry, for the edifying of the body of Christ, till we all come to the unity of the faith and of the knowledge of the Son of God, to a perfect man, to the measure of the stature of the fullness of Christ...

- Ephesians 4:11-13

We see from the above passage that Jesus gives us those with special anointings for special tasks. He even said in the above Scripture how long He would give them to us—until we all come to the unity of the faith. So the apostle and prophet anointing is needed for a while yet. These servants of God are necessary to equip the body of Christ to function properly. They have special talents to bring maturity into the body. They are to teach us and lead us in sound doctrine, and they encourage us to grow into all that the Lord has for us. We are in need of more of them in our time.

...that we should no longer be children, tossed to and fro and carried about with every wind of doctrine, by the trickery of men, in the cunning craftiness of deceitful plotting, but, speaking the truth in love, may grow up in all things into Him who is the head—Christ—from whom the whole body, joined and knit together by what every joint supplies, according to the effective working by which every part does its share, causes growth of the body for the edifying of itself in love.

-Ephesians 4:14-16

These servants of God do have special giftings for their individual offices, but many of those special talents are to give them a focus for what they have been called to do. Pastors have an anointing for shepherding the flock, apostles are sent as church planters, and evangelists are divinely gifted to share the gospel. In the modern church we have very little understanding of these offices, and we tend to believe that pastors are to do everything for everybody all of the time. Our lack of knowledge, lack of the Holy Spirit, and general apathy cause us to look to our pastor for every function of the church. We do not realize that we as believers have also been called by God to do certain things.

And He said to them, "Go into all the world and preach the gospel to every creature. He who believes and is baptized will be saved; but he who does not believe will be condemned. And these signs will follow those who believe: In My name they will cast out demons; they will speak with new tongues; they will take up serpents; and if they drink anything deadly, it will by no means hurt them; they will lay hands on the sick, and they will recover."

-Mark 16:15-18

Why are more believers not doing these things?

First of all, we need apostles, prophets, teachers, evangelists and pastors to raise us up and mentor us. We need to know how to do these things.

Secondly, we need to be obedient and do what we are told. Many times I hear someone talking about how they do not know what their personal calling is. They are praying and praying, "Oh God, show me what my special talent is." They have not even tried to do any of the things that He has commanded them to do. We need to yield to Jesus in every aspect of our lives. We need to read the Word, pray, fellowship with believers and spend time being mentored by mature Christians. If we are obedient in these things, then the above Scripture will not seem so unnatural to us. We will simply accept that if it is God's will for believers to lay hands on the sick then He must mean for me to do it. Personally.

Thirdly, and most importantly, if we are going to walk in the things that God has called us to do, then let's allow Him to do it the way He wants. Let's invite Him to come and do it Himself through us. Let's accept that He wants to fill us up to overflowing with the Holy Spirit so that we can do all of these things effectively. When they are done well, it glorifies Him.

Now you are finished reading this book, but your journey has really just begun. Today is the first day of the rest of your life. Please join me in one last prayer as you go forth into all that God has called you to.

Heavenly Father, we praise Your Holy Name and glorify You above all else. For You are awesome and worthy and we love You. Thank You, Jesus, for this day and for all that You have blessed us in and with. Glory Hallelujah! Lord, we come before You with thankful hearts for every precious gift that You have bestowed upon us. We praise You and thank You that You saved us on that cross, and that You died to set us free from all that binds us. Glory to Your Holy Name! Heavenly Father, we want to be obedient to You right now. We ask You for more of Your Holy Spirit. May You continually overflow in us in every way that You desire to.

Father, we give ourselves wholly to You. If there are any giftings that You would like to pour out on us, then we ask for them right now in Jesus' Name. Lord we know that we need more prophets, apostles, teachers, evangelists and pastors. If any of these are Your will for us, then we ask You to give us that anointing and training to do Your work and be a blessing for Your kingdom. Whatever talent You have bestowed upon us, we ask that You will use it for Your glory. We give those talents over to Your will right now in Jesus Name.

Heavenly Father, we also ask for an increased appetite for the things of God. Help us to feed our spirits and to saturate our souls with more of Your presence. We are hungry for more of You. Bless us, oh Lord, with more of You. Bless us, oh God, with rivers of juicy Fruit that runs pouring forth from our cups like a waterfall on everyone around us. May all that we do glorify You, for You are awesome!

In the Name of Jesus, may You raise up the reader of this book to all that You have called them to do. May You pour forth every blessing upon them that they need for doing Your work and Your will. May You bless their hands for their tasks and their feet to stay firmly planted on the path that You have chosen for them. I release them now in the Name of Jesus to go forth in the function and calling that You have predestined for them according to Your will. All glory be unto the Lamb. In Jesus' Name I pray and claim these things.

Amen.

About The Author

Kerry George is pastor of New Life Valley Fellowship in Black Diamond, Alberta. She is a single mother of three who also spends her time home schooling her children while she continues to complete her Bachelor's Degree through a distance-learning program. Kerry has done various speaking engagements, and ministers in a worldwide capacity to abuse victims via the Internet. Kerry has a desire to see healing and restoration in the body of Christ. Her ministry is dedicated to seeing people healed, saved and set free in Jesus' name.

Printed in the United States
1244400002B/1-51